The Book of Muhammad

IN THE SAME SERIES

The Book of Devi by Bulbul Sharma

The Book of Vishnu by Nanditha Krishna

The Book of Shiva by Namita Gokhale

The Book of Krishna by Pavan K. Varma

The Book of Ganesha by Royina Grewal

The Book of Durga by Nilima Chitgopekar

The Book of Muhammad by Mehru Jaffer

The Book of Nanak by Navtej Sarna

ALSO AVAILABLE FROM PENGUIN

The Names of Allah by Parvez Dewan

Hymns of the Gurus translated by Khushwant Singh

The Hanuman Chalisa of Goswami Tulasi Das translated by Parvez Dewan

Rehras: Evensong—The Sikh Evening Prayer translated by Reema Anand and Khushwant Singh

The Name of My Beloved: Verses of the Sikh Gurus translated by Nikky Guninder Kaur Singh

The Book of Prayer compiled and edited by Renuka Narayanan

The Book of
Muhammad

MEHRU JAFFER

PENGUIN
VIKING

VIKING
Published by the Penguin Group
Penguin Books India Pvt Ltd, 11 Community Centre, Panchsheel Park, New Delhi 110 017, India
Penguin Group (USA) Inc., 375 Hudson Street, New York, New York 10014, USA
Penguin Group (Canada), 10 Alcorn Avenue, Toronto, Ontario, Canada M4V 3B2 (a division of Pearson Penguin Canada Inc.)
Penguin Books Ltd, 80 Strand, London WC2R 0RL, England
Penguin Ireland, 25 St Stephen's Green, Dublin 2, Ireland (a division of Penguin Books Ltd)
Penguin Group (Australia), 250 Camberwell Road, Camberwell, Victoria 3124, Australia (a division of Pearson Australia Group Pty Ltd)
Penguin Group (NZ), cnr Airborne and Rosedale Roads, Albany, Auckland 1310, New Zealand (a division of Pearson New Zealand Ltd)
Penguin Group (South Africa) (Pty) Ltd, 24 Sturdee Avenue, Rosebank, Johannesburg 2196, South Africa

Penguin Books Ltd, Registered Offices: 80 Strand, London WC2R 0RL, England

First published in Viking by Penguin Books India 2003

Text copyright © Mehru Jaffer 2003
Illustrations copyright © Penguin Books India 2003

Illustrations by Subroto Mallick

All rights reserved

10 9 8 7 6 5 4 3 2

Typeset in Sabon by Mantra Virtual Services, New Delhi
Printed at Saurabh Printers Pvt. Ltd, Noida

This book is sold subject to the condition that it shall not, by way of trade or otherwise, be lent, resold, hired out, or otherwise circulated without the publisher's prior written consent in any form of binding or cover other than that in which it is published and without a similar condition including this condition being imposed on the subsequent purchaser and without limiting the rights under copyright reserved above, no part of this publication may be reproduced, stored in or introduced into a retrieval system, or transmitted in any form or by any means (electronic, mechanical, photocopying, recording or otherwise), without the prior written permission of both the copyright owner and the above-mentioned publisher of this book.

To Farrukh
my mother, whose fantastic interpretation of
Islam inspired me to find out for myself
and
to Syed Muhammad Jaffar
who never tired of repeating 'Go to
China if you must in search of knowledge'.

Contents

Introduction	1
The Birth of Muhammad	25
Pre-Islamic Arabia and the Kuraish	33
The Orphan	45
Growing up with Abdul Muttalib and Abu Talib	53
Marriage to Khadija	61
The Wives of Muhammad	69
The Revelation and Flight to Medina	75
Medina: The Ideal City	87
The Science of Biography	99
The Kaaba	105
The Five Pillars of Islam	111
The Message of the Koran	125
The Last Sermon	131
After Muhammad	135

Introduction

Once upon a time there lived a man who changed the course of history simply by being good.

Years of intense introspection finally revealed to Muhammad Abdullah of Mecca that the natural state of all human beings is goodness. And if that fundamental law is violated, the meaning of life is lost. To be good is to be kind, compassionate and charitable. And God, Muhammad believed, is the ultimate idea of goodness. Muhammad spent his own life living up to that ideal of perfection and asked others to do the same.

The Prophet's message is as simple as that. In fact, it is so simple that it is almost a disadvantage. Dr John A. Hall finds Muhammad's humanity so full-blooded that he feels the religion is too advanced for its own good. In theory at least, Hall says in *Powers and Liberties*, there is nothing to prevent human beings from trying to perfect themselves in the image of God. The very austerity, the very openness of Muslim society, he adds, makes it impossible to respect anything that interferes in man's relationship to the creator.

Muhammad himself said, 'You are all answerable to God. You have been given unlimited freedom to act as you deem fit and to forage whatever pasture you like without being answerable to anyone. Rather you shall be held accountable before your Creator for each act, each word, in fact for the whole course of your life when you have been given autonomy. You will be raised after death and presented in the court of your Lord for reckoning.'

But the way this simple message is put into practice

today is at the root of many problems.

Over time, the idea of Muhammad has come to mean many things to many people. To his followers he is a prophet, but for the vast majority he remains a mystery. About himself, he says, 'I am only a human being like you. God has sent me as an apostle so that I may demonstrate perfection of character, refinement of manners and loftiness of deportment.'

Surely Muhammad must be one of the most mesmerizing men to walk the earth, and also the most maligned. Therefore the yearning remains, even 1500 years after his time, to know more about the merchant who is remembered today as the Messenger of God. The most interesting attempt is made by those constantly trying to free the memory of Muhammad from the common cage of cliché where he is imprisoned by a past blurred with age, by legends so loving that they make him seem unreal. But Muhammad is very real. He remains extraordinary as a prophet and a leader for having realized his dream in his own lifetime. Before his death in 632 AD, he succeeded in uniting all of Arabia through his new faith. In fact, at no other time in history except for a few years at the beginning of the Islamic era has Arabia been united under a single power.

For years the different families of Arabia had felt fenced in by the encroaching influence of the Romans and Persians, the two super-powers of that time. They lived under constant fear that forces more powerful than their own cantankerous clans might colonize them one day. By uniting over 200 tribes under the banner of

Islam, Muhammad also liberated the Arabs from the confines of a peninsula that they were forced to circle for centuries in search of the most basic necessities of life. He turned the tattered tribal strength of a scattered population into a single military movement that became legendary for its might. This eventually led to the united desert tribes swarming out of the peninsula in single strength to hold both cultural and military sway over most of the world for over a millennium, beginning with Syria, Iraq, Egypt, Iran, Carthage, the Indus Valley and Spain.

At the time of Muhammad's birth Arabia was dismissed as an arid, godless zone where a wild race of people survived in small gangs in search of opportunities to plunder and loot. The Greeks called the inhabitants of this sparsely populated area Sarakenoi, or those who live in tents. Muhammad was probably saddened by this reputation planted upon his people. His broad forehead must have creased up with concern as he wondered what it was about the Arabs that made them appear so shabby in the eyes of the world.

The landscape of Muhammad's homeland, Hijaz—literally, barrier—is named after the vast, forbidding stretch of rough, treeless countryside that naturally separates it from the fertile plains to its north, east and south. There is not one river that flows from its source to the sea in the entire peninsula. Sharp, stony steppes rise knife-like from the west along the Red Sea and slope gradually eastwards towards the coast of the Gulf. To this day the amount of land cultivated in Saudi Arabia is less than one per cent. The intense heat of the plains is enough to singe anything that dares to dream of breathing and the most difficult to nurture here is hope itself. Bands of people in tiny groups have roamed the Arabian Peninsula for thousands of years, from even before Muhammad's time, trying to eke out a living literally from bare rocks, and in search of that elixir of life called water.

By the time Muhammad came of age, the city of Mecca, where he was born, had grown into an important urban centre of trade due to its excellent location in the middle of a road that went north to south from Palestine to Yemen and the presence of Zamzam, the only spring of freshwater in the vicinity that made Mecca so precious to both peddlers and pilgrims. The other roads at this junction went east to west, connecting the Red Sea coast with the route to Ethiopia and the Persian Gulf. Weary travellers broke their journey around Zamzam, discovered it is said by Bedouins in the Biblical times of Abraham. Apart from the Zamzam, whose waters are described poetically as being sweeter than honey and made cooler than ice by the constant touch of seven heavenly creatures, Mecca was also home to the Kaaba, the cube-shaped shrine built beside the holy waters and that has been sacred to the Arabs from times not recorded by history. Till the time of Muhammad the Kaaba was home to hundreds of idols and was the site of polytheistic worship for all Arab tribes.

Traders and pilgrims who constantly came here to rest, to cut a better deal and to pray also brought affluence to Mecca. The caravan trade poured great amounts of money into Mecca, but wealth also made individuals eventually very selfish. Muhammad grew up in the midst of hectic commercial activity in an urban atmosphere where wealth was worshipped in the form of idols. Most Meccans, including Muhammad, belonged to the ruling tribe of Kuraish (shark) because they had settled in the hollow of the valley around the waters of the Zamzam. But countless other offshoots of the same family continued to roam the periphery of the desert and with time were divided into numerous smaller clans that forever fought for supremacy over each other. In the pursuit of more power and wealth, people showed little compassion even for members of their own family, and it was often the more upright and less cunning that suffered the most. In the name of trade, merchants practised usury at the expense of the weakest members of society. Muhammad was pained to witness the daily intrigues practised by the elite. There were many clever ones who benefited from the unjust profits they made— profits that brought them so much wealth that they thought nothing of wasting it—while the plight of the poor worsened.

Muhammad saw in this state of affairs the ruin of his people. He wanted the wealth generated in the city to be fairly distributed for the maximum good of the maximum number of Meccans. Throughout his life he angered authorities with his insistence that the city's earnings should also benefit the most needy. Muhammad did not disapprove of riches, only the immoral and cruel deeds of the rich. He said, 'God loves the pious rich man who is inconspicuous,' and often repeated, 'The best of you are those who have the best morals.'

Immorality and cruelty was what Muhammad saw at the Kaaba. He liked to be at the Kaaba and often meditated at the shrine of his forefathers. But it upset and hurt him to see some pilgrimages performed in the nude and ritual fornication acted out at the feet of hundreds of idols. Another favourite sport of the day was to tie up the limbs of those who were helpless and no longer useful or pleasing, and leave them to broil in the naked heat of the desert sun. Since women did not often become warriors, when it was thought that too many were born they were killed. Muhammad saw fathers bury newborn daughters alive, and young girls being traded as slaves, sometimes to appease the gods. All this turned him against polytheistic worship. He was consumed with thoughts of an alternative way of expressing his spirituality and the seed of monotheism began to take root into his mind. Instead of going through complicated lanes and by lanes to seek the source of all life he began to chalk out a single, straight path of righteousness to the Creator. He gave up the adoration of all other deities as false worship apart from the only One Ultimate Reality, or God. In fact, he ruled later in his life that the greatest sin of Islam was the worship of material things and putting one's trust in idols to achieve either spiritual or worldly contentment.

Muhammad singled out monotheism as a cure for tribalism gone astray; in a time of polytheistic prayers he chose to focus all attention on one point of worship, for society as well as the individual. As Karen Armstrong writes in *A History of God*, 'Only by acknowledging him [the creator] as As-Samad, the Uncaused Cause of All Being, [would] Muslims address a dimension of reality beyond time and history and which would take them beyond the tribal divisions that were tearing their society apart.'

Muhammad felt that unity and peace were the greatest needs of his time. And none was more aware of the exigencies of his time than Muhammad himself, who predicted that a time would come when the accidental and temporary regulations would have to be differentiated from the permanent and general.

'You are in an age in which if you abandon one tenth of what is ordered, you will be ruined . . . but a time will come when he who shall observe one tenth of what is now ordered will be redeemed,' he said. Muhammad also said that religion is easy and whoever overburdens himself in his religion will not be able to continue in that way. 'So you should not be extremists but try to be near to perfection and receive the good tidings that you will be rewarded and gain strength by worshipping in the mornings, afternoons and during the last hours of the night.'

What Muhammad taught then remains relevant

now, as the moral despondency faced by Arabia in the sixth and seventh centuries seems a mirror image of our own troubled times. Apalled at all the cheating and lying around him when many a thought and action was termed relative, Muhammad tried to search out absolute values. He looked for the meaning of life and wanted to find out what it meant to be a human being. Born in an atmosphere of waste and utter urban despair, he probably feared the future, which make his personal and public concerns similar to our own. His message taught people to correct greed and corruption and he spent his own life trying to transcend human pettiness. He readily asked to be forgiven whenever he felt that he had wronged in the eyes of the Ultimate Reality he called God or even in the eyes of his fellow human beings. On numerous occasions he recited: 'Oh Allah! I am but a man. If I hurt anyone in any manner then forgive me and do not punish me.'

Overcoming greed, pettiness and learning to share money as well as experiences with each other was an absolute must if the Arabs were to prosper both politically and spiritually. Muhammad sensed the trouble brewing beyond the border of his home. There were forces far more powerful than the people of Arabia that played deadly politics at the Arabian doorstep. He saw the possibility of one greedy super-power or the other gobbling up all of Arabia if the Meccans continued to live in a world of their own. Muhammad warned the Meccans, but they seemed to have no thought for tomorrow.

Introduction

Muhammad had learnt to ask the question why from an early age. His inner world brimmed over with sorrow as he dealt with loneliness that comes from being an orphan. Why was it that his father had died even before he was born, he must have wanted to know. And where did his mother go away forever when he was barely six years old? Muhammad was born into the family of Hashim or bone breakers, named after the great number of animals the clan's ancestors were famous for slaughtering and for their unbounded hospitality in equally sharing parts of the animal with others. But at the time of Muhammad's birth the fortunes of the clan had collapsed due to counter plotting by cousins far more worldly wise than his immediate elders. It must have bothered Muhammad why a gentleman as kind and generous as Abdul Muttalib, his grandfather, was deprived of his position as top man of the Kaaba. Or why did the custodians of the Kaaba who had taken over the leadership from his grandfather were not able to fulfill their responsibility with a similar nobility and vision?

Later in life Muhammad was to repeatedly wonder why he did not have a male heir. He did have two sons from Khadija, his first wife, but both died in infancy. In the last decade of his life he married more than a dozen times and had many concubines but only one other child was born to him. Muhammad named this child Ibrahim, after Abraham, the prophet. The infant did not survive and was buried by Muhammad just a year before his own death. The Arabs call all those without a male heir an *abtar*, or incomplete. Muhammad may have suffered shame at having no surviving son and was inconsolable for many years till the message from heaven comforted him with the words, 'Yes, we have given you in abundance. So pray to your Lord and sacrifice. It is your enemy who is the abtar!'

Although born in comparative poverty, Muhammad cultivated considerable influence on his society even as a young man due to his charisma and wisdom that is said to have been beyond his years. Above all he was known to be just. His reputation as Al-Amin, or the trustworthy one, had spread beyond his immediate community and even community elders relied on his balanced council and gentle diplomacy.

Once the Kaaba was vandalized. It was robbed and damaged and the elders wondered how to repair the house of God without making any member of the mighty Kuraish tribe feel that he had been left out. The draperies of the outer walls were damaged and everyone rich and poor contributed to repair the Kaaba. When it came to returning the sacred black stone to its niche in the eastern part of the wall arguments started over who was going to perform the task.

There seemed no compromise in sight and the atmosphere became so tense that some citizens were on the verge of coming to blows when Muhammad entered the sanctuary. He cooled down tempers by asking for a cloak and placing the stone in the middle he got the representative of each clan to hold one of the four corners of the cloak. This way the stone was returned to its original place.

By the time he was twenty-five years old, Khadija, a rich widow, several years his senior, for whom he worked, asked him to marry her. Muhammad soon became a successful merchant and there was no dearth of comfort or cash anymore. If he had wanted he could have contentedly concentrated on even more women, perfume and fine clothes. Or he could have remained on top of the mountain, where he often went to meditate, high on an endless supply of peace and quiet without a care for human beings other than himself. But Muhammad was too down to earth to live in the clouds. It was while hidden in a cave that he realized that he could not live on mountain peaks forever. He needed to be around and with people.

All this while Muhammad also continued to struggle with a temperament he found troubling. He is reported to have suffered from attacks of the sort that people hostile to him dismissed as epilepsy. Maxime Rodinson in his 1980 biography writes that beneath the surface there was a temperament that was nervous, passionate, restless, feverish—filled with impatience and a yearning that seemed to burn for the impossible. This was so intense as to lead to nervous crises of a definitely pathological kind.

Muhammad's companions claim that he suffered from a chronic disease, probably high blood pressure that he treated with bleeding. There are others who debate whether it was hysteria that occasionally overwhelmed Muhammad. His psycho-physiological constitution is compared to mystics, shamans and all those who are able to sense that which is beyond the comprehension of ordinary people. Muhammad heard sounds like the ringing of bells, and voices that whispered to him. Even as he seemed to be in control of his emotions much of the time, he went through periods of great anxiety. Others found it difficult to keep pace with him as he walked like someone racing down a hill. Muhammad sweated profusely, suffered severe headaches and often went into a state of trance. He was also in the habit of washing himself several times during the day as he found body odours extremely offensive.

And when he was overwhelmed with the way that his world was, Muhammad clambered back to the naked mountains outside Mecca. He hid himself in the dark, damp womb of caves for calm. He used sweet-smelling oils such as musk on himself and routinely lighted camphor on scented chips of wood as he pondered why his own self perplexed him so much. With little thought of food or garments on his mind he dwelt for days upon the destiny of man and the awesome mystery of existence. He reasoned that if greed, arrogance and ignorance existed, the opposite of all that is cruel and vile must also be real. It must have been here, inside the cave, that the light glowing beyond the darkness of the void was first glimpsed by him. Here he must have been inspired to look for the positive of every negative. If human nature was so flawed he must have searched for the flawless, and in the midst of impermanence he must have sought the permanent.

One day he returned from the mountains a little more conscious of the existence of the permanent and the perfect. He was certain that to spend life seeking anything other than the continuing balance of opposites was meaningless and yearned to get as close as was humanely possible to this distant, but perfect idea. It is not difficult to imagine that at least some of the many adjectives used in the opening lines of the holy recitations to describe perfection may have first come to Muhammad's mind around this time. The words were eventually woven verse by verse into a text called the Koran that begins, 'In the name of God, the Merciful, the Compassionate, Praise belongs to God, the Lord of All Being, the All Merciful, the All Compassionate, the Master of the Day of Judgement. You alone we worship, You we ask for help. Show us the straight path, the path of those whom You have favoured, not of those who earn your anger, nor of those who are astray.'

Al-Lah shares a common root with the word used for power all over the Middle East for at least six thousand years. To the ancient Canaanites the ultimate power and perfection was *elat*, in Hebrew it is *elohim*, and the Aramaic word is *alaha*. All these words suggest a reality of cosmic unity, oneness and endless serenity, the supreme force behind both being and nothingness. In this word Muhammad must have grasped the mysterious concept of God—Allah—or the holy essence and found himself afloat in the void, in the unknown area between the two opposites of Al (positive) and Lah (negative).

But each time Muhammad raced down the mountains to convey what he was beginning to experience, he ended up earning the wrath and ridicule of the Meccan warlords and the guardians of the Kaaba who were from Muhammad's own tribe, but most dismissive of his philosophical temperament. It was perhaps the torment of being ridiculed as a madman that made Muhammad reluctant at first to talk openly about the Revelation when it finally came to him from God on the mountain of light. This is when the angel Gabriel told him that he was the Messenger of God. He confessed everything immediately to his wife who was the first one to convert to Islam. But for the majority of Meccans, believing in one God was a dangerous and ruinous idea. It meant the removal of the idols of all the 360 gods and goddesses that cluttered the Kaaba. It meant going against the faith of their fathers. They were afraid that the gods and goddesses whose idols were destroyed would rain anger and destruction upon Mecca. Besides, if the custodians of the holy shrine worshipped only one God what would happen to the roaring business? Profits made from pilgrims flocking to the Kaaba to pay homage to their personal gods and goddesses would dry up. No, it was decided, they must not listen to Muhammad, or allow him to brainwash others in Mecca.

❖

Those in authority dismissed what Muhammad said and hunted him out of the city. He was forbidden to pray at his beloved Kaaba and none would trade with him. For a while he lived on the outskirts of Mecca with his family, a few friends and little to eat. His uncle and guardian Abu Talib, who was head of the Hashim family, had died and the other elders of the clan had turned against Muhammad. There were plots to assassinate him. After having spent fifty-two years of his life in Mecca, Muhammad eventually migrated to the oasis town of Yathrib, 250 miles north of Mecca under the cover of darkness, after he was promised patronage and protection by a group of friendly Bedouin pilgrims who came regularly to pray at the Kaaba. The pilgrims wanted the judicious Muhammad to resolve a serious dispute between two tribes of Yathrib and the people were so pleased to find Muhammad in their midst at last that Yathrib was renamed Medinat al-Nabi (Medina), or the city of the Prophet. Muhammad's move to Medina along with a group of close companions also marks the start of the Islamic calendar.

It was in Medina that Muhammad's role as a charismatic leader was perfected. Here Muhammad had many more friends and he no longer feared opposition. Even before the migration, his belief in himself as the Messenger of God had become as solid as the rocks that surrounded him. He had succeeded in making some sense of the most important *jihad*, or struggle, within his own self. He was older and years of self-reflection had mellowed and matured him. He felt emotionally strong, and he calmed the fears of elders who warned him of dangers ahead. 'Dear uncle, do not go by my loneliness. Truth will not go unsupported for long. The whole of Arabia and beyond will one day espouse its cause,' he said to an elder while still in Mecca.

All those concerned about his safety constantly pleaded with Muhammad to give up his impossible mission. But he told them that even if the sun were placed in his right hand and the moon in his left, to force him to renounce his work, he would not desist 'Until Allah manifest His cause, or I perish in the attempt'.

All the confusion that had clouded his life in Mecca dispersed by the time he decided to build the utopia of his dreams in Medina. The verses revealed to him in Mecca provided him with spiritual guidance. In Medina Muhammad laid the foundation on which to build an individual's moral character. He brought morality out of the dark corners of monasteries for practice in daily life. He asked the merchant to be moral and the policeman to be pious, if only for the love of God.

The machinery needed to create an ideal community of people was assembled in Medina. It was thought important to work within institutions to eliminate the constant fear of mutual violence. The hope was that a stable and secure home (state) would prevent the undoing of the Arab people. What Muhammad did in Medina was to boldly turn his back on the tribal society of his ancestors and to experiment with a modern, urban way of life without negating his past in total. He took what he thought was the best in the morality of the

Introduction

nomad and adapted it for settled communities. Ideally he would have liked to modernize Mecca itself, but the danger to his life from some members of his own family was so real that it was Medina that was first converted into a living example of a perfect Muslim society where the population became so upright that doors did not need to be locked.

Muhammad felt deeply inspired in Medina mainly because of an extraordinary intellectual understanding that he had gained about himself at this stage in his life. He refused to leave it all to hallucinations and began to put into practice everything that he liked to preach. In Medina, Muhammad introduced social reforms and moral standards far higher than those prevalent in his time. Not everyone agreed when Muhammad said that life was sacred in its entirety and not just at the time of prayer, but he had learnt to face opposition. 'When a man prays publicly in a good manner and prays secretly in a good manner, God most high says "This is my servant indeed",' Muhammad repeated tirelessly. He told his companions that it was his tongue that he feared most and insisted that righteousness was good character and sin was that which revolved in the heart and which one did not want people to know.

Muhammad established a religious and social model that the diverse population of Medina could follow, and his message first found a framework here. Policies were developed and concrete institutions formed within which it became possible to resolve spiritual as well as social problems faced by the people of that time. With the consensus of all residents of a cosmopolitan Medina, including pagans, Arabs, Jews, Christians and Muslims, a written constitution came into being where the rights and duties of individuals were defined, the customary private justice was abolished and the liberty of religion was granted to all. And slaves were freed.

One of the first things that Muhammad did on arrival at Medina was to build a mosque. This place of prostration was a simple structure with a roof made from palm leaves. Muhammad stood on a tree trunk to lead the prayers and to preach. Equally humble-looking structures sprung up around the mosque where Muhammad lived with his family and friends. Here Muhammad demanded that each one must be good, as a command from God. He is remembered as having questioned, 'Do you love your Creator? Then love your fellow beings first.'

Since Muhammad met everyone who came to see him in his humble home, the women in his family put a curtain between their private place of rest and the part of the house where numerous visitors were welcomed. The women made this arrangement on their own. Muhammad did not order them to lose themselves inside layers of cloth. He did not want to hide them or for them to remain oblivious about the world they lived in. Muhammad loved women. He was proudest of Khadija, his first love, and he adored his daughters. However Muhammad did suggest modesty to a sister-in-law once: 'Oh Asma, when a girl reaches puberty it is not proper that anything of her should remain exposed except this and this,' he said, pointing to her face and the palms of her hand. But he enjoyed being with women and women accompanied Muhammad everywhere, including to the mosque. A quote from his wife Aisha reveals that she went to the mosque and prayed along with Muhammad as she stood in the row of women nearest to the row of men.

Muhammad always encouraged the generous giving of alms. He said, 'He is not a perfect Muslim who eats his fill and lets his neighbour go hungry.' He not only talked of equality amongst all human beings but was also always the first to practice it. During a journey it is reported that his caravan stopped to rest. His companions divided the chores amongst themselves to prepare a meal. Muhammad chose to collect the firewood. When his companions pleaded with him not to trouble himself he said, 'I do not like to attribute any distinction to myself. Allah does not like the man who considers himself superior to his companions.'

To Muhammad's contemporaries he was a worthy leader to emulate. He was a brilliant military strategist, and above all, commanded an even greater moral authority. His wisdom lay in delegating responsibility of administration to the right person. His sense of justice was such that even all those hostile to his teachings flocked to him in search of impartiality. When a well-known member of society was found guilty of theft Muhammad waved aside all petitions on the influential person's behalf to overlook the crime, saying, 'Many a community ruined itself in the past as they punished only the poor and ignored the offences of the exalted. By Allah, if my daughter Fatima would have committed theft, her hand would have been severed.'

While trying to search out the essence and truth of his own life, Muhammad also kept a close watch on the needs of those around him. This was the special magic of Muhammad, a prophet but who was also an extraordinarily lovable leader of his people. He is great because he was able to share his selfless ideas and feelings in such a way that his followers discovered that they were the ones to benefit most from becoming Muslims.

The state of Medina became an ideal form of governance, where children especially were taught to go in search of knowledge, for that was considered to be the right path to God. 'People are like mines of silver and gold, the more excellent of them in the days of ignorance are the more excellent of them in Islam when they attain knowledge,' said Muhammad. Many people, especially women, fled elitist, tribal Mecca in hordes as new laws in Medina promised equality and dignity for all, whether man or woman, master or servant.

But many of the refugees in Medina were often homesick for Mecca. Aisha, Muhammad's young wife, found her elderly father Abu Bakr sometimes depressed and sick with longing for home. One day Amir and Bilal, two former slaves, were running a high fever, and Bilal in his delirious state but haunting voice sang of the day when he would once again spend a night in Fakhkh with sweet herbs and thyme around him. Would the day dawn, he sang, when he would see the waters of

Majanna and Shama and Tafil again? When Aisha talked about the sadness that occasionally overcame the community, Muhammad prayed that God would make Medina one day as dear to them as Mecca was, or even dearer. For Muhammad himself missed Mecca as much as the others, if not more.

In Medina the image of Muhammad as politician and military leader magnified larger than the man. Here he was likened to a just oasis in a desert dotted with the unjust. Soon the number of followers in Medina increased from a handful to thousands of believers who finally returned to Mecca in 629 AD to pray at the Kaaba without any resistance from his enemies. Muhammad is considered the best of all creatures for having cleared the way for all humanity to better the self and for not caring about the risks to his life in doing so. Muhammad fought a few battles while in Medina. He lost some and won others, but his most triumphant jihad remains the one that helped him conquer the quarrels and contradictions that raged inside his own self.

Medina remained a model city-state until 644 AD when the rule of the second successor after Muhammad came to an end. After that, most Muslim leaders have found it difficult to practice the ideals of Muhammad, precisely because they are so simple. The ambition of every leader, even today, remains to be crowned king and to be left alone to enjoy the temptations of Turkish delight and Mogul mania despite Muhammad's own warnings: 'What I have forbidden to you, avoid, what I have ordered you to do, do as much of it as you can. It was only their excessive questioning and their disagreeing with their prophets that destroyed those who were before you.'

Just before his death in 632 AD, Muhammad announced the perfection of the new religion he preached based on the message he had received from God in the form of the Koran. He gave it the name of Islam, or surrender of the self, and all those who willingly surrender to no other god but the only God have ever since been called Muslims, both words derived from the same word *salaam*, or peace. They number over one billion people around the world today and include both Arabs and non-Arabs.

The Birth of Muhammad

Muhammad was born to Amina Wahab in 570 AD in Mecca, a city cradled between a range of black and yellow mountains where the waters of the Red Sea flowed far below their stony feet. Some say it was in the year of the elephant when the Christian ruler of Yemen attacked the Kaaba. The army of the enemy is called the people of the elephant in the Koran. The unarmed Abdul Muttalib, leader of the Meccans, custodian of the Kaaba and grandfather of Muhammad, watched helplessly that day as the enemy marched towards them. The Meccans had never seen elephants before and they were afraid of the gigantic animals. They followed the example of Abdul Muttalib and went into deep prayer while it was loudly announced that the Kaaba, the boast and glory of Meccans, would soon be destroyed. Abdul Muttalib replied, 'The House you propose to demolish is not mine . . . but you should know that it has a master Almighty to protect it.'

When the army reached the Kaaba, the crowds that had gathered were amazed to see the men insist but the animals refused to go further into the sacred place. And all those who remembered the spectacle later said that a great sandstorm appeared out of nowhere and the skies were covered with a flock of hundreds of ababil, or little birds, that clutched poisonous pebbles in their feet and beaks. These pebbles were released upon the enemy, some of whom died instantly while other soldiers suffered painful skin eruptions. Ibn Ishaq, the first biographer of Muhammad, wrote in the eighth century that the image of the Kuraish shone brighter than ever in the eyes of all those who witnessed Abdul Muttalib face the enemy astride the huge animals with nothing except prayers.

Muhammad was brought up on this loving legend of the elephants. Another poetic version of Muhammad's birth describes the proud mother holding her newly born baby in bony arms, rubbing frail fingers over the infant's handsome brow as if to iron away wrinkles of worry from the baby's soft skin. Amina whispered Ahmad, or one who deserves to be highly praised, to her son.

It is believed that every mountain on that joyful morn echoed the tidings to other mountains and together they chorused that there is no god but God! Seventy columns of light were erected in heaven and earth, each a ray of different colour. After the baby was washed seven times and perfumed, Gabriel, the angel, stood at the door while countless other angels filed in to salute the last prophet of time. And by divine power the chamber enlarged to accommodate one and all who entered saying, 'Peace be upon you, oh Muhammad! Peace be upon you, oh Mahmud! Peace be upon you, oh Hamid! And peace be upon you, oh Ahmad!'

A cloud is said to have overshadowed the Kaaba, showering down saffron, musk and amber. Every idol fell on its face and the wise dreamt that a number of strong camels were leading the horses of Arabia across the Tigris. On that night in every holy book of the world a drop of blood appeared to signify that Muhammad would be a prophet armed with a sword. And on the altar of every monastery and hermit's cell was written,

The Birth of Muhammad

'Know that the untaught prophet is born'.

The throne of every king was reversed, the skill of soothsayers departed and the magic of sorcerers ended. Satan shrieked as he heard the glad tidings, and was chained and imprisoned in a tower where he wept for forty days.

According to scribes, Satah was a celebrated soothsayer just before the birth of Muhammad. Described as a body of flesh he had few bones except for a skull. Satah spent his life incessantly surveying the heavens. He hardly slept and lived rolled up like a garment. Nothing moved except his tongue and eyes and he preferred to be carried, unrolled and laid out on a mat before kings when they wanted to confide their secrets and to consult him.

One night as he studied the heavens he saw lightning on the horizon. The stars were ablaze and dashed against each other to fall on earth. Smoke went up in columns and Satah felt blinded and quivered at the spectacle. Next morning he asked to be carried to the summit of a high mountain. As he gazed around the heavens he was amazed by the light that he saw engulfing the horizon and was overwhelmed by the prodigies he witnessed. He knew that his death was near and the time had come for the prophet from the clan of Hashim to be born. Satah declared, by the everlasting Lord who sustains the heavens without pillars and by the unity of the supreme Eternal One, that a son would be born to

Abdullah to impart religious guidance to men and to lead them in the way of truth, righteousness and goodness. And he would destroy idols and unite all worshippers. Asked to describe the prophet, Satah said that he was an illustrious person, an apostle from the Lord of glory who will soon arise and whom the tongue of Satah was unable adequately to describe.

> He is of medium and agreeable stature, and adorns a mark between his shoulders. He will wear a burden and his prophetic office will continue till the Judgement Day. In the dark, light will beam from his forehead and when he smiles the lustre of his teeth will illumine the world. A person of such perfection has never yet walked the earth. His discourse is charming, and in devotion and abstinence from evil he is unequalled. He is not proud and imperious. He will always speak the truth, and give a correct answer to those that interrogate him. His birth will be legitimate and pure and free from any ancestral taint. To believers he will be benevolent and to his companions kind. His name is conspicuous in the Torah and Gospel. He is the balm of all affliction and renowned for his generosity. His name in heaven is Ahmad and on earth Muhammad.

On hearing Satah speak, all those who wished him well in Mecca immediately bound him upon a camel

The Birth of Muhammad

and begged him to leave before those angered by his prophecy brought harm to him.

In *Fazaeel* (or *Excellencies*), Sharan-bin Jibraeel says that on the night of Amina's conception glad tidings roared throughout the seven heavens. After a month, mountains and trees, heavens and earth whispered the news to each other. Three months later a man named Abukabafah was returning from Syria, and on approaching Mecca his camel placed her head on the ground and prostrated. The man struck the animal with a stick and a voice called him by name, saying, 'Smite her not; do you not perceive that every creature except mankind is prostrate in adoration, and rendering praise to God that three months have passed from the conception of the untaught prophet? You will soon behold him; woe, then, to the worshippers of idols on account of his sword and the swords of his companions.'

Each month after that was marked by similar prodigies till the ninth month saw angels from all the heavens descend down to earth, each bearing a lamp of light unfed by oil. On each of the ten thousand angelic lamps was written: There is no god but God; Muhammad is the apostle of God. In the second volume of *The Life and Religion of Muhammad*, Muhammad Baqir al-Majlisi, leading authority on Iranian narratives and expert in religious sciences in the seventeenth century, writes that in this bright array the angels encircled the sacred city of Mecca.

As Amina waited in her chambers, the roof of the house opened and four heavenly bodies entered to light up the place with their radiant presence. The tender virgins of paradise soothed Amina's fears. They attended upon her till Muhammad was born at dawn on a Friday on the seventeenth day of the third month of the Islamic calendar, 7900 years, four months and seven days after the death of Adam, the father of all mankind.

Yet another source says that Muhammad was born exactly 9900 years, four months and seven days after Adam.

Pre-Islamic Arabia and the Kuraish

Just before Muhammad was born, the rich and fertile kingdoms of the southern parts of Arabia had lost their independence to the super-powers of the day. The Romans in the north-west were Christians, and in competition, the non-Christian Persians in the east befriended the Jews. The various Arab rulers of southern Arabia (present day Yemen) were sometimes puppets of the Romans and often of the Persians. The Meccans sided a little more with the Romans than with the Persians. In 510 AD, six decades before Muhammad, the ruler of Yemen had converted to Judaism and was patronized by the Persians. But by 525 AD the same king was unable to keep Christianity at bay and soon fell to Abyssinia (Ethiopia) that had already embraced the Roman Catholic faith.

The Arabs in the heart of the peninsula were extremely proud of the agriculturally lush land to their south that was believed to be the original area mentioned in the Old Testament as the Garden of Eden and were saddened to see it colonized. They were now afraid for their own security as they watched foreigners march up so close to their own caravan. In *Powers and Liberties*, Dr John A. Hall writes, 'The intrusions of the two empires that surrounded Arabia, Byzantium and Persia had recently increased: these were exceedingly irritating to the Arabs who were united by strong ties of ethnic identity. These two empires were possessed of monotheistic religions, and it is quite possible that some Arabs felt inferior in the presence of stricter and more respectable belief systems.'

Since Mecca was a bustling bazaar and had emerged as the most important centre of pilgrimage in all of Arabia, the Bedouin was absolutely petrified of losing his city and his independence like the Arabs of the south. He was desperate to safeguard his home. The city of Mecca was a detour on the overland trade routes linking the Mediterranean with southern Arabia and the Indian Ocean. Traders rested their caravans in the holy land without fear of being harassed or attacked as people here were known for their deep-rooted hospitality despite the hardships. 'Qualities such as manliness, valour, generosity and hospitality are valued highly; even the intertribal raids, and the vendettas which occurred whenever blood was shed were conducted according to precise if unwritten rules,' says Colin Turner, lecturer in Islamic Studies and Persian, University of Durham.

Arabs like the Syrians had converted to Christianity under the influence of the Romans and their sedentary way of life with a complex cuisine and culture was considered superior to the Bedouins that did not even have a written script of their own. The great powers of the day were the settled kingdoms of Byzantium (present day Turkey) under Rome, and Persia (present day Iran). The Bedouin of the Hijaz in central Arabia was in awe of the naturally fertile fields and the man-made pomp and glory that glittered like a necklace around the very bare lands of his ancestors. Looking upon his own dusty existence he was often filled with doubt and some shame. Despite his pride in his tribal way of life, he questioned his spirituality and wanted to know why Al-Lah or the

God had left him to fend the elements of life for himself without friend, philosopher or prophet? And the fact that he was found forever engaged in bloody feuds, very often with his own relatives, brought to his mind a picture of himself that was not very flattering.

Those Bedouins who were involved in regular trade with the affluent worlds of the Romans and Persians returned home with tall tales about the king and kingdoms that had flowered around the stark existence of the Arabs. The Bedouin perhaps realized that he could never hope for similar power and prestige as long as differences between tribes diluted the strength of a united Arab front. He began to dream of pooling together the life force within all individuals to convert it into one deep and wide ocean. He started to search for everything that was common amongst the Arabs and fantasised over facing the world as a community of one people, under a single authority, a concept that he was vaguely but already aware of. The Arab society was after all divided into numerous clans that were caught in an endless cycle of wars and vendettas with one bloody feud inevitably leading to another. Most tragic was the fact that all the conflicts and killings invariably involved people from the same family.

The community of the Bedouin was arranged in tribal kinship units, based on real or imaginary descent from a common ancestor through the male line, in order to combat the dangers of daily life. All economic, military and political activity amongst both settled as well as the nomadic population revolved around a tribe.

Whatever the quality or quantity of the loot of the day, it was always shared equally amongst all members of the tribe. This was the positive aspect of tribal life. Most of the time there was so little to go around that the leader rarely found any surplus to hoard for himself. The tribal chiefs therefore enjoyed much power and influence but they were seldom wealthy. Every inter-tribal relationship was forged through alliances or feuds that took place naturally and routinely over scarcity of food, water or animals. Since feuding was such an important part of every tribesman's life and battling enjoyed absolute social approval, all tribesmen were also warriors, with the more tough nomads being far more adept in battle than those belonging to communities that were settled. It was a common practice to loot the trade caravans of other tribes that led to a continuous chain of brutal attacks on each other.

Tribal loyalty and repeated reconfigurations through marriages, amongst smaller clans especially, helped to prevent the emergence of larger political units or economic cooperation. Human life was lived here in the midst of very precarious conditions and the worst enemy was hunger. This reality brought people closer but also made populations compete fiercely with each other over the most basic necessities of life.

Since it was impossible to plant anything on the land, trade was the only profession the Bedouin could indulge in. And every journey through the dangerous and dreary wasteland was undertaken under the protection of a *kafilah* or a caravan that included children and animals. This was necessary for mutual defence and comfort. Each caravan travelled with a chief who was chosen by the group that could number from ten people to thousands with a corresponding number of camels, horses, mules and donkeys carrying loads of goods or people.

A tribe is always considered one big family where people are related to each other. Arabia did not have a government with a king or president in those times as it was impossible to keep track of a largely wandering population. The elder members of the family helped to settle quarrels between individuals and disputes over injustices. At that stage of Arab development, there was no notion of a universal, natural law. Each tribe prided itself on its own special brand of *muruwah* or honour that is inherited by blood. The Arab ideology of muruwah is described by Armstrong, a comparative religions scholar, as courage in battle, patience, endurance in suffering and a dedication to the chivalrous duties of avenging wrong done to the tribe, protecting its weaker members and defying the strong. To preserve the muruwah of the group, each member has to be ready to leap to the defence of a fellow tribesman and obey his chief without question. Outside the tribe this obligation ceases and, often, an 'anything goes' kind of behaviour takes over.

As custodian of the Kaaba, the Kuraish was the most influential tribe at the time of Muhammad's birth, although the riches within the family were fast on the decline. The Kuraish paid homage to three moon goddesses, al-Lat (bright moon), al-Manat (dark moon) and al-Uzza (a combination of the light and dark), considered the daughters of Banat-al-lah, the high god. The worship of idols was mainly phallic, similar to the ways of ancient Semites, but the devotees had reduced the adoration of their respective gods to crude fetishism. Human sacrifices were common and among some tribes a camel was killed on the tomb of a beloved one or allowed to die of starvation in the belief that the beast was needed by the dead as conveyance in any future existence. Yet the Kaaba was different to all the other temples in the vicinity for more reasons than one and also the most prestigious as it was the chapel of Abraham and Ismail, and before that of the Biblical Adam, the Saturnian father of all mankind. Here the tribes came year after year to kiss the black stone which had fallen from heaven in the primeval days of Adam and to circuit the temple, often naked. Apart from pagans even the monotheist Jews and Christians sent offerings to the shrine. The custody of this temple therefore was the object of great jealousy throughout the peninsula as Arabs conferred upon the custodians much honour and privileges.

As populations multiplied, the Kuraish who traced their ancestry to a single patriarch branched out into groups of several clans over a period of many generations. It is the cleverness of the founding fathers of the Kuraish that Mecca was eventually converted into a mercantile city of great importance. By the end of the sixth century, some of the richest merchants of Arabia belonged to Mecca and the city had become a powerful magnet for both merchants and mendicants who came here in search of the most exquisite wares brought by the best craftsmen from far and near.

The fame of the Kuraish spread across the length and breadth of the desert as devout caretakers of the holy shrine as well as smart tradesmen. The tribe made most of its money from buying and selling to the pilgrims who came in caravans with camels carrying heavy loads of gold, food, incense, leather and cloth. The accompanying horses and donkeys were mounted with lighter bags that went to Yemen in the winter and to Syria in the summer. In the hope of a safe and profitable journey of every caravan, the traders routinely prayed at the Kaaba along with the Kuraish.

It is said that the city of Mecca never slept. For 365 days it hustled and bustled with the coming and going of an endless flow of pilgrims and peddlers joined by tinkers and tailors, the rich and the poor who together helped to light up the crevice hidden in between the lower ends of rocky mountains with so much life that it remained like a lone star twinkling bright on the otherwise barren face of an endless wasteland. A century before the birth of Muhammad the Kuraish had given up the nomadic life and settled in Mecca. Various members of this family were still breeding stock but they were also involved in trade and made money as caretakers of the holy shrine at the Kaaba. The Kuraish basked in all the power and influence enjoyed by them. They were admired for playing politics in a very clever way and respected for being kind. In the rivalry between Rome and Persia, they did not take obvious sides and tried to tame the wild temperament of their fellow Bedouins from the outskirts of Mecca by employing them as soldiers to guard the city.

The Kuraish had formally declared themselves as the people of the shrine through a religious association called the Hums. They distinguished themselves from the Bedouin by wearing different clothes and head dress and were known never to leave the shrine. The reputation of Abdul Muttalib, Muhammad's grandfather, grew as a generous provider of food and water to plenty of pilgrims and tired traders. It is he who converted Mecca into a safe haven where all forms of violence was forbidden. He is also responsible for having rediscovered the holy spring of Zamzam. By the beginning of the seventh century, the Kuraish had left their old nomadic ways and hunger was like a bad dream from the past. Everyone in Mecca in fact was most content in the knowledge that they did not have to fear enemy tribes lurking round the corner to harm them.

But a few decades of peace and prosperity also began to dull the minds of a fast growing elite and a certain amount of nonchalance made its way into the daily lives of the people. It became increasingly obvious that in the process of making more and more money the old communal tribal ethic was being practised less and less. Some Arabs, more sensitive than others, saw beyond the glitter and glamour of the capitalist success that Mecca had become. They began to miss the generosity

Pre-Islamic Arabia and the Kuraish 43

and dignity involved in the egalitarian way of life of the past. They felt saddened to see greed and self-centred individualism take off from where the community ways of the nomad had ended. Many head of a family had formed his own clan and all the different clans were in cut-throat competition with each other. By the time Muhammad reached puberty there were three main rival clans that had clamoured to the top, as if of a pyramid, and tried to outdo each other in terms of wealth, power and glory while the rest of the population lay with little at the bottom.

The clan of Hashim into which Muhammad was born was no longer in charge of Mecca. The utter humility of the Hashimites was in stark contrast to the obnoxious arrogance of the Omayyids, who had succeeded in usurping the custodianship of the Kaaba from the Hashimites. The Omayyids were powerful, but not respected. The resentment against them grew as they shamelessly piled up all the fortune for themselves alone. There was little attempt at sharing equally what was earned according to the tribal ethic of yesteryears. There were many who made money at the expense of the very poor in society and Abdul Muttalib now lived a life of extreme modesty in the autumn of his life.

'Their new prosperity had severed their links with traditional values and many of the less successful Kuraish felt obscurely disoriented and lost. Naturally the most successful merchants, bankers and financiers were delighted with the new system. They aggressively accumulated more capital with near religious zeal. Only two generations away from the penury of the nomadic life, they believed that money and material goods could save them and they wanted as many of these things as they could get. But some of the younger generation were growing disenchanted and seemed to be searching for a new spiritual and political solution to the malaise and disquiet in the city,' explains Armstrong.

Thus, the society into which Muhammad opened his eyes was on the verge of moral disintegration and very vulnerable to foreign invasion.

The Orphan

Just as she had sensed during her pregnancy that she was carrying no ordinary child, Amina also knew that life was not going to be easy for her son. Abdullah, her husband, was already dead and food was forever scarce in the home of all those belonging to the clan of Hashim. Amina was a daughter from the family of Zuhrah, a clan of richer merchants, but the fortunes of Abdul Muttalib, her father-in-law, had declined towards the last years of his life. And by the time Amina gave birth to Muhammad the family had fallen on difficult days. In a power-struggle within the Kuraish, Abdul Muttalib had lost the custodianship of the Kaaba to his cousin Omayya. This happened despite the use of all diplomatic efforts by Abdul Muttalib to live in harmony with all those who had differences with him. As the most important member of his clan he had tried to maintain peace by marrying several women belonging to many other clans. Altogether he had fathered ten sons. The historian Ibn Saad quotes Meccans as saying that among the Arabs the sons of Abdul Muttalib were the most prominent and stately of profile. The youngest of them was the one dearest to his father. He was called Abdullah and his face had a radiance that the other brothers did not have, handsome as they all were. Abdullah, Muhammad's father, is said to have left behind him the most fragrant trail of amber and musk. He was nicknamed Lamp of the Sacred City and it was his luminous beauty that lit up all of Arabia.

After the birth of Muhammad, Amina was so undernourished that she had to look for a wet nurse.

But none wanted to nurse her baby as he did not have a father to pay for the services. Amina was seven months in the family way when Abdullah had died on his way back from Medina, where he had gone on a business trip, leaving her just one slave, five camels and a few sheep.

Amina finally found Halima, a woman even poorer than herself, to take care of Muhammad. The same year that Muhammad was born the lands of Arabia were afflicted with a famine and a terrible drought and the nomads roaming the outer regions beyond the hollow of the valley now flooded into Mecca desperate for work and food. Halima was from the Saad clan, belonging to one of its poorest families and had travelled to Mecca with a group of ten other women in search of making money. She reluctantly agreed to nurse Muhammad whose family, she realized, had little to offer her by way of compensation. When Muhammad was first brought to Halima she said, 'An orphan! And with no money! And what can his mother do?'

Soon all the other nine women had found babies to nurse and returned home, except Halima who asked her husband, 'What do you think? My companions have gone and there is no boy left in Mecca to nurse except this orphan. Shall we take him? I should not like to return home with nothing.'

The husband said, 'Take him! Perhaps God will make him a blessing to us.'

Halima herself is quoted as telling an ancient scribe, 'I went and took the orphan . . . and when I laid him in my lap he looked in my face with light beaming in his eyes. He took my right breast and nursed a whole hour but refused the other breast that he left for my own son, and by the blessing that attended the infant prophet, I was able to supply both the children. On carrying him home milk began to drop from the distended udders of our impoverished camels that now yielded a sufficient supply for us and for our children. My husband said, "You have taken a child that has brought a blessing along with him."'

On the way back from the valley the caravan passed a cave out of which came a man, the light of whose forehead shone to heaven. He saluted the Prophet and said that he was appointed by the most high to attend and protect him. A flock of gazelles likewise approached and said, 'Oh Halima do you know whom you wait? He is the purest of the pure.' Every mountain and plain that they passed saluted the child.

Halima reported that the condition of the family and the cattle improved with each day after that. While the sheep and camels of the others returned hungry from the pasture, Halima's were always well fed.

The years of his early childhood spent in the pure air of the countryside and away from the pollution and noise of Mecca did Muhammad a lot of good. It is also at this time that a mystical experience mentioned by different authors at different times in Muhammad's life is said to have occurred. One day Muhammad asked Halima where his foster brothers went each morning, and when she replied that they went to graze cattle, he said, 'I will go with them today.'

But Muhammad's foster brothers were alarmed when Muhammad was suddenly whisked away by strangers that day. These strangers turned out to be two angels who laid him down on his back, and using a wing as a sword opened Muhammad's breast to take out his heart. A drop of blood was extracted from his heart and it was further cleaned with water brought from paradise. The heart was again dipped in a basin of red rubies to wash it of all doubt and uncertainty before being returned to Muhammad's breast. He was then put on one side of a scale and thousands of people sat on the other side, but Muhammad's side remained heavier, making one of the angels say, 'Let it be. Even if you brought the whole community of Arabs to the scale, he would still outweigh it.' This incident is a symbolic act of initiation that appears in most religious texts for all those around the world who are ritualistically purified to receive a sacred message.

Meanwhile, the other children informed Halima that Muhammad was missing and she went to look for him everywhere. And when at last she found him, she pressed him to her bosom, showered him with kisses, and asked, 'What happened to you?' Muhammad replied, 'Fear not, dear mother, God is with me.' And at that moment Halima inhaled perfume more fragrant than musk all around her.

Halima was puzzled and frightened after the incident and immediately took Muhammad back to his mother.

The Orphan

After hearing Halima's story Amina told her that Muhammad was no ordinary child and that he had a great future waiting for him. Amina recalled the moment when Muhammad was born. She had heard many voices that had no human semblance. She had seen a banner of silk from paradise mounted on a staff of rubies that filled all the space between heaven and earth.

'I saw many birds around me, and a youth appeared, taller, fairer and more elegantly dressed than I had ever seen before. He took my son and dropped into his mouth some saliva from his own and said, "Remain in the safe keeping and guardianship of God, Verily I have filled thy heart with faith, knowledge, mildness, certainty, understanding and heroism. Thou art the best of mankind, happy is he that obeys thee, and woe to him that opposes thee." This mysterious person then produced a white silk purse and taking from it a signet ring impressed a seal between the shoulders of the child, and said, "My Lord has commanded me to breathe into thee the Holy Spirit." He then put upon the babe a shirt, saying, "This is thy protection from the calamities of the world."' The seal between Muhammad's shoulders was seen by many others who talked about it later and some have left the information in writing.

Muhammad now with Amina in Mecca after having spent a few precious years traversing the magnificent desert with Halima whose caravan was found pitched in a different corner of Arabia every other day. Many years later when Halima found Muhammad again and knocked on his door, he immediately recognized her and cried, 'Mother, mother!' He promptly fetched his cloak and spread it out so that Halima could sit on it. After that whenever his Bedouin parents came to see him, Muhammad always gave them a gift of either food or cattle.

Growing up with Abdul Muttalib and Abu Talib

Muhammad was six years old when Amina travelled with him to Medina to visit her family and to stop by her husband's grave. On the way back, Amina suddenly died. Having lost both his parents at so tender an age, Muhammad went to live with Abdul Muttalib, his grandfather. Abdul Muttalib preferred to call him Muhammad instead of Ahmad, the name given to him by his mother. However, Mahmud, Hamid and the other names of Muhammad, including Ahmad, are all derived from the same root—*hamd*, meaning praise.

Abdul Muttalib showered the child with much love, but he too died two years later, leaving Muhammad an orphan once again. Muhammad was now the responsibility of Abu Talib, who had succeeded his father as head of the Hashim clan.

Muhammad's grandfather had loved him dearly. He took the boy every day to the Kaaba where he spent his last days lying on a bed in the vicinity of the holy shrine. Muhammad was to remain deeply inspired by the generosity, gentleness and majesty of his grandfather for the rest of his own life. He never forgot Abdul Muttalib's single minded and brave opposition to the corruption of his times. Muhammad himself confessed later that he had included several meritorious principles into Islam that he had observed his grandfather practice. Muhammad found it most appropriate that while his grandfather was custodian of the Kaaba, Abdul Muttalib should have made it illegal for Meccans to marry a woman who had been his father's wife. Some other practices advocated by Abdul Muttalib which also left a mark on Muhammad and which he incorporated into Islam were the giving away regularly of a certain percentage from one's personal treasures purely for charitable purposes, and the imposition of a fine of one hundred camels for slaying a man.

Muhammad was impressed that it was his grandfather who was responsible for having rediscovered the Zamzam and dug out the precious spring of water for the benefit of all.

It was at this spot where Hajara, according to the Old Testament, had left the infant Ismail crying incessantly as she went in search of water. Ismail had cried out in thirst and repeatedly rubbed his little heels in the sand till water sprouted beside the baby as if by magic in the very heart of the vast wasteland. When Hajara saw a spring of water gurgling beside her infant son, she excitedly exclaimed in Egyptian, 'Zem, zem (stay, stay).'

When Ismail was still a child and lived here alone with his mother Hajara, members of the nomadic Jurhum tribe strayed into Mecca in search of water. They asked Hajara's permission to drink from the Zamzam and presented Hajara with a couple of sheep as a token of gratitude. Ismail was happy to play with the young ones of the nomads. The Jurhum became regular visitors to the site and later settled down in Mecca. Hundreds of years later when the Khuza took over the Kaaba, the Jurhum were forced to flee but not before they clogged the waters of the Zamzam with swords and stones.

It was Abdul Muttalib who was asked in a dream

to dig up the spring so that its waters might never fail to furnish an endless supply for the pilgrims. But on waking up he had no idea what was meant by the dream. For three consecutive nights he received the same command and on the fifth morning saw a white winged raven picking ants at the precise spot where he began digging for the well.

Abdul Muttalib had only his son Haris to help him and they did not stop digging till they found the spring. When water finally spluttered out, Abdul Muttalib cried, 'God is great!' When the other Kuraish saw the water they promptly came to claim a share in the successful enterprise but Abdul Muttalib sent them away saying, 'You did not assist me in the work, the well therefore belongs to me and my sons down to the day of judgement.'

Muhammad also chose seven as the number of circuits to be performed around the Kaaba, earlier not limited by any rule before Abdul Muttalib. It is obvious that the mystical meaning of seven was not lost on the elderly gentleman who used it as a symbolic path to absolute perfection and to God. Abdul Muttalib must have pondered over the seven planets at equal distance rotating in the same direction and their sacredness, and was inspired to make circling the Kaaba seven times suggestive of the eternal harmony of the universe, similar also to the seven colours of the rainbow and the seven notes in music. Just like his grandfather, Muhammad got into the habit of retiring for the entire month of Ramadan to the caves in the mountains where he spent much time, his meditations being interrupted only by travellers who stopped by to share with Muhammad their meagre provisions and thoughts.

Some scribes say that Abdul Muttalib was 120 years old when he died and the leadership of the clan of Hashim passed down to Abu Talib, Muhammad's uncle, born from the same mother as Abdullah, Muhammad's father. When Muhammad came under Abu Talib's care, he was eight years old.

Abu Talib was so protective of his nephew that he took the child wherever he went. One sweltering hot summer's day Abu Talib led a caravan to Syria. He was advised to leave Muhammad behind in Mecca to beat the heat, but did not want to be separated from the child. He mounted Muhammad on a camel that strode in front of his own so that he could keep a constant eye on the child. Abu Talib is quoted as saying that as soon as the heat of the sun became oppressive he saw a small cloud as white as snow make an umbrella over the child and cast a most refreshing shadow from above. During that journey, none of the leather bottles in the caravan were ever found empty of water and the camels always came across excellent pastures to graze.

When they reached Basra, an important stop and meeting place of five caravan routes and the centre of Christianity, a hermit called Bahira came running to greet them and is said to have broken his silence for the first time in his life. The monk was not known to speak to anyone and had the reputation of not letting the hustle and bustle around him ever disturb his contemplation. But that day, seeing a blinding light and its rays reaching up to the heavens before him, the hermit emerged out of his meditation and charged ahead to find out what was going on. He saw the cloud above the child that sparkled like a diamond and knew that the Prophet had arrived as predicted in the holy book. The tree under which the caravan rested was shrivelled and devoid of leaf. As Muhammad took his place beneath the dead tree, it suddenly shook and swayed and became verdant. Leaves sprouted on numerous boughs and three kinds of fruit—two eaten in the summer and the other one found only in winter—dropped down for the weary travellers. A tank that had been dry since the Jews rejected the Christian apostles now filled up. The prophecy was that when water was seen again in the tank it would be by the blessing of the Prophet who will be born in Mecca and flee to Medina. Among his own people he will be called Amin, and in heaven Ahmad. He will be of the posterity of Ismail, the son of Abraham.

Bahira brought a humble portion of eats for Muhammad who shared it with the entire caravan. After all the 170 people had had their fill, Bahira's plate seemed not to have been touched. The hermit asked if he could look in between Muhammad's shoulders, where he spotted the seal of prophecy. He kissed the head of Muhammad and cried, 'By the truth of Lord Christ this is he! I see what you do not and know certain things unknown to you. Take this child under the tree whom if you knew as I know him, verily you would take him on your shoulder and carry him back to his native city. All those who see him will recognize him as I have done by the marks he bears and treachery will endeavour to destroy him . . . The Arabs and Persians will obey him, voluntarily or involuntarily.' Bahira left with tears of joy in his eyes.

On another journey to Damascus, Abu Talib says that the wisest of the wise came to Muhammad and one called Hestoor stayed for three days and nights without speaking a word. Finally he too asked to see Muhammad's shoulder, and on spotting the birthmark promptly kissed him. At that time Muhammad was about nine years old, and according to some scribes the opening of his breast and the purifying of his heart actually took place at this time.

Marriage to Khadija

At the age of twenty-five, Muhammad was a fair-complexioned, handsome man, but was still a bachelor, probably because he could not afford a wife. Stories about Muhammad's miraculous ways and examples of his honesty soon reached Khadija, a rich widow who was forty years old and managed a booming business in export and import. Khadija's curiosity was killing her. She wanted to see the man whose praises she heard sung by the whole town. She asked her minions to seek Muhammad out and finally when he stood before her she felt that she had seen him before. She wondered where.

Then she remembered the evening when she had been advised to bathe in waters charmed by incantations, to tuck a special prayer under her pillow and retire for the night if the promise that she would soon dream of her future husband was to be fulfilled.

In her dream she had seen a person of medium height with a thick curly beard and long hair. He was of sturdy build with tapering limbs and fingers. His forehead was generous and he had large, black eyes. His eyelashes were long and lush, his nose sloping, his mouth somewhat large and his teeth well set. He wore a pleasant smile as he had galloped towards her on a horse of light, astride a saddle made of gold and holding a golden bridle in his hand.

There was a birthmark between his shoulders and this horseman came out of the house of Abu Talib. When he came close to her, Khadija embraced him and seated him on her lap, after which she woke up and could sleep no more for the remaining part of the night.

When Muhammad, the man of her dream, entered Khadija's house, it is said to have glowed with his refined presence. Khadija was already looking for someone trustworthy to buy expensive merchandise for her from Syria. Business had often suffered in the past when her caravans had been attacked and goods stolen and looted. She was impressed with the impossible role that Muhammad was famous for—as mediator between more than 200 warring tribes, each one festering with a jealousy and strife more lethal than the sword they carried. She just felt safe about surrendering her business to Muhammad.

Working with Khadija presented Muhammad with an opportunity at last to earn a decent income and also to restore to the tribe of Hashim some of the power and glory that it had enjoyed during the lifetime of Abdul Muttalib. He took the job offered to him and was immediately presented with two camels, new clothes and bags full of gold and silver coins. Khadija was so charmed by Muhammad that she gave him her own she-camel, celebrated for its beauty and speed, for his personal use.

Muhammad returned from Syria with great profits for Khadija and those who were part of the entourage told her about the many miracles they had witnessed on the way. She was told that Muhammad had seen them safely through a tempest. On another occasion he had raised his hands heavenwards in prayer and a spring of water had gurgled out from the burning sand beneath his feet. A serpent as large as a very tall tree of dates

Marriage to Khadija

had moved out of the way of the caravan and offered salutations of peace. Just before they arrived in Damascus, a learned, old monk had hurried out of a large monastery and wept with joy and called Muhammad the last prophet mentioned in the gospel.

Khadija was already attracted to the way he looked, and his fabulous reputation, modesty, good character and honesty only added to the charm. She asked Muhammad what he would do with his share of the profit earned from the successful mission to Syria. Muhammad replied that his uncle's advice was that he should use the money he had at last earned to get married. Khadija smiled and asked Muhammad if she should help him find a wife. When he agreed, Khadija said that she had a woman in mind from a family as illustrious as his own and who surely excelled all other women in Mecca in wealth, beauty and generosity. She would happily support Muhammad for the rest of her life. But she had had two husbands who were dead and she was older to him.

When Muhammad figured out that Khadija was proposing marriage to him, he drowned in perspiration and did not know what to say. For a moment Khadija feared that he would turn down her proposal of marriage. But with great humility Muhammad replied that Khadija was rich and that he was poor. He deserved a wife equal to his own humble status. Khadija said, 'Whatever is mine is yours. Will one who gives you her heart refuse you her property?'

Khadija was fifteen years older to Muhammad when

they married, but from that day till the end of her life two decades later there was no other woman in Muhammad's life except her.

Khadija and Muhammad ran a happy household of many children and an endless flow of family and friends. Khadija was a mature woman of the world with an independent income. She had been married twice before and was the mother of several children. It will be no exaggeration to say that Muhammad basked under her loving care and generosity. But he did not know how to indulge himself in the riches of the world. He kept an open house and shared everything with all those who had less. He was grateful not to have to struggle anymore for a home and hearth, and spent all his leisure time in further introspection. Now Khadija too accompanied him into the mountains on the outskirts of Mecca where Muhammad liked to meditate, and Ali, his young cousin (son of Abu Talib), went with them everywhere. After a severe famine that had further strained the finances of Abu Talib, Muhammad had asked his uncle to let the five-year-old Ali live with him. Together with Zaid, the slave Khadija had gifted Muhammad on their wedding but who refused to return to his parents even after Muhammad set him free, Ali grew up in Muhammad's home as his own son.

All those jealous of Muhammad's sudden good fortune kept a close watch on him. He was taunted when the first child born to him was a girl, and once he had three girls his rivals publicly called him abtar. The rebuke of those around him perhaps made Muhammad mourn even more for the two sons that were born to him but did not survive. Khadija was almost sixty years old when Fatima, their fourth daughter, was born. Some Islamic scholars interpret the birth of Fatima and the special relationship that she shared with her father as a miracle and quite prophetic. Fatima is seen as the motor force of the revolution that Muhammad introduced into Arab society. While other members of his tribe founded dynasties and conquered kingdoms in the name of Muhammad, the memory of frail Fatima remains to this day as the only spiritual heir to the legacy of the Prophet. No man is known to have showered as much love and respect as Muhammad did upon Fatima. He proudly kissed Fatima's hands and cheeks in public and declared that the best women in the world were four: Mary (mother of Jesus Christ), Asiah (wife of the Pharaoh who brought up Moses), Khadija and Fatima.

Muhammad had this to say about little Fatima:

> God is satisfied with her contentment and becomes angry from her anger. The contentment of Fatima is my contentment, her anger is my anger. Whosoever loves my daughter Fatima loves me. Whosoever makes Fatima content makes me content. Whosoever makes Fatima unhappy makes me unhappy. Fatima is a part of my body. Whosoever hurts her, has hurt me, and whosoever hurts me, has hurt God.

Earlier a woman did not inherit anything from her family except a lifelong regret for being alive. Fatima is believed to have inherited the essence of what Muhammad was trying to say and do. Fatima is loved to this day for being one of the few to have followed in her father's footsteps to the end of her life. Through the family of her children, Hasan and Husain, her followers founded the Fatimid Dynasty that ruled large parts of North Africa, including Cairo, between 909 AD and 1171 AD and which tried to emulate the virtues of modesty and humility as practised by Fatima. The role that the memory of Fatima continues to play in keeping alive the spirit and values closest to Muhammad's heart is yet another defiance of the savage tribal tradition of giving importance only to male heirs. It is the Fatimid rulers who chose green as the colour of Islam in a symbolic allegiance to Ali, Muhammad's cousin and husband of Fatima, who had wrapped himself in a green cover and laid down in place of Muhammad to abort an assassination attempt on the life of the Prophet.

Muhammad compared himself to a tree, Fatima to the trunk and Ali to its pollen. Hasan and Husain were called the fruits of the tree and their followers its leaves. Today all those who claim their faith and ancestry from the children of Fatima and Ali are known as Shia Muslims and it is believed that only through them Muhammad continues to have descendants.

The Wives of Muhammad

After the death of Khadija, Muhammad is said to have been beside himself with sorrow. He is said to have entered the grave himself to lay her in it. Although Khadija was much older to Muhammad, the marriage was a happy one. Syed Amir Ali writes in *The Spirit of Islam*, 'The marriage brought him that repose and exemption from daily toil which was needed in order to prepare his mind for his great work, but beyond that it gave him a loving woman's heart that was the first to believe in his mission, that was ever ready to console him in despair and to keep alive in him the thin flickering flame of hope when no other man believed him and the world was black before his eyes.'

Khadija was no doubt the most important person in the life of Muhammad. She is the first to believe in Islam and in Muhammad as the Messenger of God. She is the one who provided Muhammad with the confidence to preach his message publicly. The several wives that Muhammad brought home after the death of Khadija are a favourite topic of discussion among admirers and critics of Muhammad, particularly his marriage to Aisha when she was just nine years old compared to his fifty-two years. But all the later marriages seem to be motivated more by the politics of the day, in the hope of a male heir perhaps, rather than lust. Most of the women Muhammad married were either widows or slaves who had converted to Islam and needed protection and patronage from those who mattered in society.

Muhammad married Sauda a few months after Khadija's death. Sauda had become a destitute after the death of her husband, who had converted to Islam and was forced to flee from the Kuraish to the friendly kingdom of Ethiopia where he had died in exile. At that time marriage was the only way a poor woman could find protection and Muhammad agreed to take care of Sauda after her husband died as a defender of Islam. Moreover, polygamy was not considered as evil as it is now. In fact, it was common practice to take as many wives as men wanted to.

Three of Muhammad's other wives were also widows. Hafsa lost her husband in the Battle of Badr between the Muslims and the Meccans. None would take her in their home because of her fiery temper and tongue, but Muhammad did, and those around him approved, even applauded him for his magnanimity. Muhammad also married Jews and a Christian out of love for sure, but above all, as a gesture of goodwill and friendship.

His marriage to Zainab is considered the most sensational of them all, as also the one with little Aisha who was given to Muhammad in marriage by none other than Abu Bakr, her father. Zainab was the beautiful wife of Zaid, the not-so-good-looking slave and later adopted son of Muhammad. It is Zaid who could not suffer the vain ways of Zainab and let her go to live with Muhammad, and the incident made little difference to his devotion to the Prophet.

Muhammad married several other women in an attempt to make friends with warring tribes and in the name of peace and unity of the Arab people. And often

The Wives of Muhammad

he found it a Herculean task to keep all his wives happy in the harem. The effort proved as difficult a process as nation-building if not more. For an unhappy wife often meant the end of peace and unity at least with the clan that the lady belonged to.

It is Muhammad who made sure that as Muslims women should inherit a share in the parents' property along with the brothers and that they are never forced into marriage. He was born in a society of ignorant warriors where female infants were buried alive. Women were considered idle consumers and their dainty physique a return of no investment during times of war. Even poets eulogized in their lyrics that the son-in-law most beloved to all fathers was the grave. A son was valued more in this society as he was seen to bring bread for the tribe while a daughter only ate it.

Muhammad tried to change the attitude of the Arabs towards women by conveying to them the true will of God. In the Koran it says, 'He hides himself from the people of the evil for the tidings given him. Should he keep her with disgrace or bury her alive in the dust? Behold, evil is what they decide.' The patriarch is consoled in the Koran with, 'Do not kill them from fear of poverty for We will provide for you and your children.'

Egypt-born Leila Ahmed the author of *Women and Gender in Islam*, feels that practices sanctioned by Muhammad in the first Muslim society reflect far more positive attitudes than became current during the later eras when the practice of concubines became widespread and access to slaves led to women being treated as commodities, with upper class women becoming increasingly marginalized. She feels that if the ethical voice of Islam is listened to it can significantly temper the extreme gender bias of the current laws.

Muhammad pointed out to the Meccans how precious women are to Arab society. He reminded them of Hajara, the only woman to be buried in the Kaaba, the first house of God. He said that Hajara was a slave but most beloved to her husband Abraham. She is the mother of Ismail, the father of all Arabs, and did devotees not remember this when they performed the sacred circumambulation around the grave of Hajara as they went around the Kaaba itself?

Muhammad's legacy is positive towards women which unfortunately has been distorted in many Islamic societies today.

The Revelation and Flight to Medina

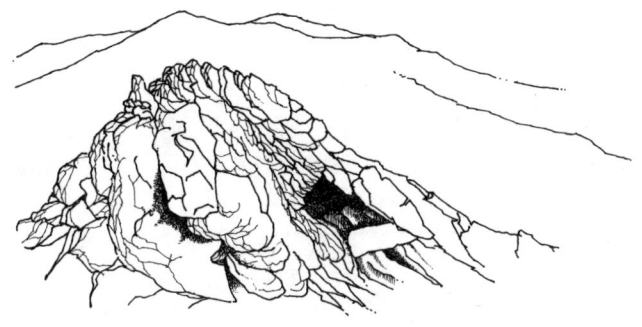

The fifteen years after Muhammad's marriage with Khadija are described by Syed Ameer Ali in *The Spirit of Islam* as a silent record of introspection, preparation and spiritual communion for Muhammad. The seeds of Muhammad's faith in himself as the Prophet finally blossomed with the Revelation. He was forty years old and it was the fifth consecutive year of his retreat to Mount Hira into the cave of research when angel Gabriel found him and told him that he was chosen as the Messenger of God. Sweating profusely and trembling like a leaf in a duststorm, Muhammad returned to Khadija to tell her how he was embraced three times by Gabriel and repeatedly commanded to recite in the name of the Lord who creates man from a clot. When Muhammad had replied to Gabriel in panic that he had no idea what he should recite, the angel said, 'To recite for the Lord most generous, who teaches man what he does not know.' When Muhammad repeated his question he received the same answer. And it was in the third attempt that Muhammad found himself reciting in the name of God that there is no god but the only God, the very first lines of the Koran. It is this simple but profound experience that elevated Muhammad, a mere dreamer of dreams, to a prophet.

The Prophet was left with no tradition from the past that could help him interpret his experiences and he was quite distrustful of soothsayers. Yet he was confused at the intensity of the holy vision in the cave and frustrated at not knowing what he should do next. All manner of thoughts clouded his mind. He wondered if he was just another magician, or a roadside miracle maker. And when he did not receive any answer that convinced him, he felt that he did not want to live any more. The thought of the embrace by the angel that had left him breathless continued to bewilder him and he was filled with despair at the thought that he might be just imagining the experience.

One day he rushed out of the cave and climbed higher up the mountain with the aim of throwing himself down to his death. The Prophet recalled later that midway up the mountain he heard a voice from heaven saying, 'Oh Muhammad! Thou art the prophet of God and I am Gabriel.' When he raised his head towards the heavens to see who was speaking, Muhammad saw Gabriel standing in the form of a man with feet astride the horizon. The Prophet stared at the spectacle as if he were turned to statue and when he could bear the vision no more he began to slant his face away from the brightness that was more blinding than the sun at daybreak. But in whichever direction he looked, he saw the apparition as before. After that Muhammad often saw Gabriel or sensed his presence when the angel returned to recite to him the message of God.

The Prophet later confessed that it was a difficult experience, and even painful, each time the Koran was revealed to him verse by verse for the following twenty-one years. He said that he never once received God's word without thinking that he was being ripped apart from his soul. After every encounter with Gabriel, Muhammad crawled to Khadija, sometimes on his hands and knees, like one seized with convulsions. Khadija would then hold him till he shivered no more, reassuring him that God would never mislead or mock him. Khadija was never in any doubt that her husband's experience on the mountain was divine and that Muhammad was indeed the Prophet. She was the first one to convert to Islam.

Except for Khadija and his young cousin Ali none other was told about the divine revelation. The two years following the Revelation were full of pain and confusion for the Prophet.

Then one day out of the blue he received the morning verse and was compelled to recite:

> Thy Lord has neither forsaken thee nor hates thee and the last shall be better for thee than the first.
> Thy Lord shall give thee, and thou shalt be satisfied.
> Did He not find thee an orphan, and shelter thee?
> Did He not find thee erring, and guide thee?
> Did He not find thee needy, and suffice thee?

The Prophet was now ready to preach publicly. At first he spoke only to members of his family and to those members of his tribe who were friendly to him.

After Khadija it was Ali who converted to Islam, followed by Zaid and Abu Bakr, an influential Kuraish. Once Abu Talib saw them in prayer and questioned

Muhammad, 'Oh son of my brother what is this religion you are following?' Muhammad answered, 'It is the religion of God . . . the pure religion of our ancestor Abraham. God has sent me to His servants to direct them towards the truth. My uncle you are the most worthy of them all . . . accept the truth and help in spreading it.'

'Son of my brother, in the true spirit of the sturdy old Semite, I cannot abjure the religion of my fathers, but by the Supreme God while I am alive none shall dare to injure you,' said Ablu Talib.

Then turning towards Ali, his son, the patriarch asked what religion was his. 'Oh father, I believe in God and His Prophet and go with him,' answered Ali. 'Well my son,' said Abu Talib, 'He will not call you to anything save what is good. So you are free to go to him.'

Soon the number of Muhammad's followers rose to thirty and they amazed the Kuraish with their intense faith and conviction in Muhammad. He tried his best to wean the other Kuraish away from their wanton ways but they laughed at him. One day Muhammad climbed the hill of Safa to warn his tribesmen of their folly in not heeding the words of all the preachers that had come before him. He invited the crowd to accept the faith of their forefather Abraham who in truth was not a Jew, neither a Christian, but one who had surrendered himself (Muslim) to his Creator and one of pure faith (Hanif). This kind of talk was too abstract for the Kuraish but humbler pilgrims from outside Mecca were impressed and wanted to know more.

Muhammad described all unbelievers as deaf, dumb and blind. He pleaded with them to think of the future and to beware of the day of judgement when the children they had buried alive would ask them for what crime were they put to death. He talked of the day when heaven and earth shall be folded away and none but God will be near, of the rewards and punishments that awaited everyone in the life hereafter. The Kuraish were incensed as some members of their own tribe became followers of Muhammad, and he was accused of turning brother against brother. But most of the converts to Islam came from less influential members of society who felt no risk could make life any worse than their immediate, miserable existence. When the majority of Kuraish refused to listen to him, Muhammad went with his message to strangers and to the pilgrims who came to Mecca for trade and pilgrimage. As the number of people who thronged to Muhammad increased, the Kuraish became openly abusive and cruel. They prevented Muhammad from praying at the Kaaba and pelted him with stones. They spread rumours that Muhammad was nothing but a dangerous magician.

Abu Talib rebuked his tribesmen for their injustice and intolerance. The elderly patriarch may not have converted to Islam himself but he admired his nephew as the most trustworthy Meccan around town and an earnest social reformer. Although he disagreed with Muhammad's religion he defended him with true desert chivalry. 'A honourable man has adopted a certain religion, why persecute him? For it is only the Lord of the Heaven who can read the heart of man!'

The Kuraish tried to tempt Muhammad with titles and riches. He refused and proclaimed that the best richness is the richness of the soul; the best provision is piety; the most profound philosophy is the fear of God, the Exalted, the Great.

His followers, who were mostly poor and ordinary people, were now tortured and killed. They were dragged to lie on burning hot sand, heavy stones tied to their chests and molten iron poured over them. One follower who was imprisoned wrote, 'Hunger has brought on such dizziness that, if at night I kick at a soft and wet material, without even realizing it, I put it in my mouth and suck it. Two years later, I still do not know what it was.' The most famous of all the faithful is Bilal, the African slave who is also the first muezzin of Islam. Bilal's master Omayya had made it a habit of dragging him each day into the plains when the heat of the sun was at its peak. A large stone was placed upon his chest and he was left on his own, unable to move. The only word that Bilal repeated during that time was, 'Ahadun, Ahadun (one God, one God)'. While other slaves were killed, Bilal was bought by Abu Bakr and freed. Muhammad arranged for some of his followers to seek refuge in the neighbouring Christian kingdom of Abyssinia.

The Kuraish decided to kill Muhammad. However, the plot that threatened to wipe out the entire clan of Hashim leaked out. Abu Talib called Muhammad and together with other clansmen hid in a long, narrow mountain quarter on the eastern side of Mecca that was cut off by rocks from the city. Here Muhammad lived in isolation with his companions for three years. The Kuraish ordered that none should marry into the clan of Hashim or do business with them. And a formal ban was imposed upon Muhammad who was treated like an outcast.

Khadija, once the richest in Mecca, became weak with starvation while in exile. She sighed one day, 'If only my approaching death could wait until these dark days pass and I could die with hope and happiness.' She would soak a piece of leather in water and hold it in her mouth when she was unable to control hunger.

'I am not worried about myself,' she said to her daughters who were constantly by her side. 'No woman amongst the Kuraish has tasted the blessings that I have. There is no woman in the world to receive the generosity that I have received. It is enough for me that my fate in this life, in this world, has been to be the beloved wife of God's choice. As to my fate in the other world, it is enough that I have been among the first who believed in Muhammad and that I am called "the mother of his followers".' Then whispering to herself, she continued, 'Oh God, I cannot count the blessings and kindnesses that you have given me. My heart has not grown narrow because I am moving towards you, but I do wish to be worthy of the benefits you gave me.'

Both Khadija and Abu Talib died within a few days of each other, reminding Muhammad that he was an orphan once again. However, they had lived to see the ban imposed by the Kuraish being lifted.

All these years, Fatima was a silent spectator to the sufferings endured by Muhammad. After the death of her mother and after her three older sisters returned to the homes of their respective husbands, Fatima stayed with Muhammad and comforted him. She was eventually called umm al-Abiha, the mother of her father.

The time after the death of Khadija and before he left Mecca for Medina is considered to be the saddest and most lonesome in the entire life of Muhammad. Traditional biographers believe that even God's heart went out to him and he was invited to visit the heavens for solace. Muslims say that on the night of the Miraj or Ascension, Muhammad had a vision of himself being transported from Mecca to Jerusalem by the angel Gabriel. In the vision, he ascended each heaven, step by step, meeting earlier prophets like Jesus, Moses, Abraham and Adam at each stop till beyond the seventh heaven he got a glimpse of God. Muhammad brought back the gift of the namaz, or the prayer recited five times a day by Muslims, from that journey. The grand vision, full of glorious imagery and seeped in deep meaning, is described in the Koran: 'Praise be to Him who carried His servant by night from the sacred temple to the temple that is more remote, whose precincts we have blessed, that we might show him some of our signs for He is the Hearer, the Seer. And remember we said to thee, verily thy Lord is round about mankind; we ordained the Vision which we showed thee.'

The Revelation and Flight to Medina 85

Although the official ban against him was lifted after three years, the Kuraish continued to hurt and hound Muhammad. But the spiritual experience of the Ascension revived his faith in himself. Muhammad's sublime trust in God was strengthened and the grandeur of his character never stood out more prominently than at this period, records history. After Khadija's demise, although he was sad at his personal loss, he drowned his sorrow in the hope that truth would triumph in the end to help all humanity.

Turned away by the Meccans, Muhammad continued to converse with traders and pilgrims, and many from the neighbouring town of Yathrib were struck by his earnestness. Those who were inspired went home and brought back others to listen to Muhammad. One day some of the Yathribites took a pledge to believe in one God, not to steal, not to commit adultery, not to kill children, to abstain from calumny and slander, to obey the Prophet in everything that was right and to be faithful to him in weal and in sorrow. This is known as the famous pledge of Akaba, named after the hill where it was taken, and those who had participated in it returned to Yathrib to spread the word about their new faith.

Soon a group of seventy-five people invited Muhammad to their dwelling in Yathrib. Homeless amongst his own tribe, he readily accepted. Having heard whispers that the Kuraish planned a massacre of all Muslims, Muhammad got them to escape to Yathrib before he did. Several assassins meanwhile surrounded the home of Muhammad in a bid to sheathe their swords simultaneously into his bosom as he slept in the thick of the night. But it was Ali who lay in bed instead of Muhammad that night beneath a green garment while Muhammad escaped from Mecca with Abu Bakr. As scores of horsemen chased him, he hid in a cave south of Mecca. Plants are said to have sprouted on the spot and spiders hurried to spin an endless web over the mouth of the cave. When Abu Bakr was still fearful and whispered 'We are but two', Muhammad replied, 'We are three. God is with us.'

Medina: The Ideal City

It was a blistering hot day in July 622 AD, when Muhammad arrived in Yathrib to a tumultuous welcome. Fatima was already there to welcome him along with other members of the family and his close companions. Ali walked all the way from Mecca after having escaped the wrath of the Kuraish when they found him in bed instead of Muhammad. His hosts were so delighted to see Muhammad in Yathrib that they renamed it Medinat al-Nabi (or Medina), the city of the Prophet. The flight of Muhammad from Mecca to Medina is called the Hijrat and marks the beginning of the Islamic calendar.

Medina woke up to a new dawn after the arrival of Muhammad. He politely refused to stay in the home of any one of his followers for the fear of creating rivalry amongst them. Instead he immediately helped to build a mosque, a common ground where members of even warring tribes met and forgot their feuds in the brotherhood of the new faith. Muhammad made his own home near the premises of the mosque. He composed a treaty called the constitution of Medina under which he organized a time for prayer, including one at noon and Bilal, the freed African slave of Abu Bakr, was made responsible for reciting the *azaan* or call to prayer. Muhammad outlined the rights and duties of all the residents of Medina and suggested that each well-to-do family from Medina adopt one Meccan and share half their belongings and property with the migrant population.

'Fraternize in the name of God. You are brothers,'

Muhammad encouraged. He got everyone, including Arabs, Jews, Christians and pagans, to work together. The result was the metamorphosis of Medina into a new Muslim commonwealth with its own constitution that above all else celebrated a more compassionate way of life.

Muhammad worked to weld together the heterogeneous and conflicting elements of the city and its suburbs into an orderly confederation. The constitution has been carefully preserved in the writing of Ibn Hisham and reveals the real genius of Muhammad. His biographers call Muhammad a mastermind not only of his own age but of all ages. 'No wild dreamer bent upon pulling down the existing fabrics of society but a statesman of unrivalled powers who in an age of utter and hopeless disintegration . . . set himself to the task of reconstructing a state, a commonwealth, a society upon the basis of universal humanity,' writes Amir Ali. The constitution of Medina provides numerous provisions to improve life for its citizens, including that all future disputes between those who accept the charter shall be referred, in the name of God, to the Prophet. This helped put an end to the anarchic and bloody custom of Arabs relying on vengeance and justice to resolve grievances.

The poetic and abstract revelations of Mecca were replaced in Medina by very practical and specific guidelines that Muhammad said were communicated to him through God to better the life of human beings. Believers were asked to avoid all forms of usury and society was told to always temper justice with mercy. In Medina, general Koranic principles and injunctions were provided for Muslims in the hope that the people will themselves interpret them in a meaningful way according to their needs and abilities.

Muhammad was happy at home. It was in Medina that the marriage of Fatima with Ali was solemnized. There were many who wanted to take Fatima as a bride, including Abu Bakr and Omar, but Fatima wed Ali who earned a living as a water carrier. The simple ceremony was performed over a plate of dates and plenty of prayers, to the music of Bilal's voice that reminded the faithful never to forget to worship. When Muhammad found Fatima in tears at having to leave his side, he comforted her. 'I am leaving you with a person of the strongest faith, a man who is the most knowledgeable among those with knowledge, the most ethical among those with ethics and the highest of spirits among the spiritual,' he said.

In the third year of the migration from Mecca to Medina, a boy was born to Fatima and was named Hasan. After Muhammad recited the call to prayer into the infant's ear, he added, 'The generation of each Prophet was from his own body but mine is from Ali.' A year later Fatima gave birth to Husain. Muhammad was obviously overjoyed and never shy of showing it. He was often found on the floor, on his knees, while his grandsons climbed on his back to ride piggyback.

In Medina, his sermons concentrated much upon the virtue of charity. He defined charity as every good act. 'Your smiling in your brother's face is charity. An exhortation addressed to your fellow men to do virtuous deeds is equal to alms-giving. Putting a wanderer in the right path is charity, assisting the blind is charity, removing stones and thorns and other obstructions from the road is charity, giving water to the thirsty is charity,' Muhammad said. The charity of the tongue is something that Muhammad himself practised, and when a follower asked him for a great rule of conduct, Muhammad immediately answered, 'Speak evil of no one.'

In the midst of teaching, and the practice of courtesies of daily life like the saying and returning of salutations to each other, Muhammad continued to face trials and tribulations that come from being the leader of an ever swelling crowd of followers. In Medina, Muhammad was forced to rise above the role of just a preacher. As head of the state he assumed the role of a general too when the time came to prevent the city from being attacked by its enemies. Much against his will and inclination, Muhammad organized his followers for purposes of self-defence to take up arms against any attack upon Medina. Finally when the Meccan army marched with a force of 1000 men towards Medina, 300 Muslims confronted them in the valley of Badr. The ensuing battle is described as fierce and swift after which the Meccans fled, having lost seventy men while seventy others were taken prisoner. The morale of the Muslims soared high after the Battle of Badr. They believed that they had been victorious against the mighty Meccans only due to divine intervention.

The prisoners were however freed after a few days and Muhammad instructed his men never to molest harmless residents, not to demolish the dwelling of civilians or fruit trees, and never to touch a palm tree with a sword. Such acts of kindness for his enemy, especially those who had been most cruel to him, did not fail to impress Muhammad's friends and foes. When he found Muslims quarrelling over the spoils of war, a new law was immediately enforced that left the division of the spoils to the discretion of the head of state after one-fifth share was deposited into the public treasury to support the poor and weak.

The Meccans returned a year later in an attempt to avenge the defeat at the Battle of Badr with an army of 3000 men. The Muslims again met the enemy with 700 men at the feet of Mount Uhud when many lives were lost and Muhammad was wounded. But Medina remained untouched. Muhammad spent the following year consulting with his companions on how to better defend Medina. Salman al-Farsi, a Persian Muslim, suggested that a trench dug around the city would keep it safe and convinced the Muslims to dig a moat for twenty days and nights. The Meccan army tried to cross the trench surrounding Medina for thirty days without success and returned without a war. After these battles the mood of the Meccans remained gloomy as they saw more and more of their people flee to Medina to live with Muhammad.

It was seven years since the refugees had been banished from Mecca and most of them missed their place of birth. Above all they craved to perform the pilgrimage and prayers at the Kaaba. And the most homesick of them all was Muhammad himself. One day, close to the approaching season of the annual pilgrimage, Muhammad announced that he wanted to return to Mecca. A thousand voices were raised in agreement with Muhammad and hectic preparations were made for the pilgrimage. But on the outskirts of Mecca the Kuraish refused to allow Muhammad to enter the Kaaba. The Muslim caravans were pitched at Hudaibiya where Muhammad preferred to make peace with the Kuraish rather than declare war upon them. After much negotiations, conducted through many messengers running back and forth between the Kuraish and the Muslims, the Treaty of Hudaibiya was signed and it was decided to end all hostilities for ten years. The Muslims had to be satisfied with prayers offered only in the periphery of the Kaaba. They chose not to force the Kuraish to allow them to perform the pilgrimage that year but came back the following year at the same time.

In the meantime some closest to Muhammad were disappointed and even annoyed at the extreme moderation and magnanimity shown by Muhammad at a time when the Muslim morale and army seemed at the peak of its strength. Watching Muhammad turn the other cheek to the Kuraish who were the cause of so much pain and suffering to the Muslims made some of his companions turn against Muhammad. The more impulsive ones even talked of a munity against Muhammad. They saw Muhammad's overtures of peace

Medina: The Ideal City

at Hudaibiya as a humiliation. Muhammad took the rebuke in silence and turned to God for consolation. At that time it was revealed to Muhammad, 'Surely We have given thee a manifest victory that God may forgive thee thy former and thy latter sins, and complete His blessings upon thee and guide thee on a straight path, and that God may help thee with might help.' This revelation is known today as the Victory Verse.

Once back in Medina the months that followed were spent in sending letters and emissaries outside Arabia, including to the Khusro of Persia and the Caesar of Rome, in an attempt to explain to the world the message of Muhammad. And all those who worked with Muhammad eventually realized the nobility of his character, endurance and above all his earnestness and fiery enthusiasm for the truth that he preached. He sent Ali on a mission with the advice, 'When two parties come before you for justice do not decide before hearing both.'

Muhammad continued to reveal himself as quite a hero in Medina, the master whom it was impossible to disobey and impossible not to love till his dying day. As more and more women and men got to know Muhammad they devoted themselves to him body and soul, and the enthusiasm caught fire and spread among other tribes, till all of Arabia was finally at his feet.

In 630 AD when the Muslims returned to perform the pilgrimage in Mecca a year after the Treaty of Hudaibiya, it was Muhammad's greatest triumph—he led 10,000 Muslims to pray at the Kaaba. By this time the Kuraish had lost all will and influence over their people. They offered little resistance to the Muslims who regained Mecca without bloodshed, marking the end of Muhammad's participation in all bloody jihads. This is exactly how he had prayed his homecoming would be. Fot it was never the intention of Muhammad to destroy the Kuraish but to eventually convince them to join him out of their own free will. Abu Sufiyan, from the rival Omayya clan and head of the Kuraish, begged for mercy and was pardoned. In fact Muhammad declared a general amnesty and gave strict orders that no blood should be shed. 'What treatment do you expect from me?' Muhammad asked of the Kuraish. 'Thou art a noble brother, the son of a noble brother,' replied one of them.

'This day there is no reproof again,' Muhammad said. This way Muhammad conquered not just Mecca but also the heart, mind and soul of the people, ending the bloody cycle of attacks and counter-attacks between the Muslims and the Kuraish.

William Muir notes that although the city of Mecca had cheerfully accepted his authority, all its inhabitants had not yet embraced the new religion nor formally acknowledged his prophetical claim. Perhaps he intended to follow the course he had pursued at Medina and leave the conversion of the people to be gradually accomplished without compulsion.

The news of Mecca's conversion to Islam spread around the peninsula faster than a sandstorm and tribe after tribe came to pay tribute to Muhammad and embrace the new faith till all of Arabia had converted to Islam in Muhammad's own lifetime. After regaining Mecca, Muhammad journeyed back to Medina to spend his last days in his adopted home. Muhammad was now getting weaker in body but his spirit glistened in serene strength. He continued to work till he found it difficult to walk and one day appeared in the mosque on the arm of Ali. Abu Bakr was asked to lead the prayers instead.

After his last prayer in public he asked to rest in Aisha's house, next to the mosque. Once there, he laid his head gently in the lap of this eighteen-year-old wife and fell asleep, forever. He was sixty-two years old.

The Science of Biography

Everything that is known about Muhammad falls within a school developed as the science of biography. The historical information about his life that is handed down by biographers is known as the Sira. The daily sayings and discourses are collected in the form of numerous Hadith or narrations as noted down by his companions. And together the Sira and the Hadith, the word of man, make up the Sunnah or the moral examples set by Muhammad in his own life. The Koran is the Revelation, the word of God and together with the Sunnah forms the theoretical and practical aspects of Islam.

Not knowing how to read or write, Muhammad had forty-five reporters making constant note of everything he said and did after he began to preach. There are over 300 documents that include political treaties, military intentions, and assignment of officials and state correspondence on tanned leather. Muhammad's later life as the Prophet is literally an open book with minute details of how he spoke, sat, slept, dressed, walked, and of his behaviour as husband, father, nephew, towards women, children and animals. The Muslims have always had written evidence of what Muhammad was like. *Sirat Rasul Allah* by Ibn Ishaq is the earliest biography written a hundred years after Muhammad's death.

It is the daily discourses of Muhammad from the time he received the first revelation in 610 AD till his death twenty-three years later that are called Hadith. One of Muhammad's many reporters was a young lad called Malik Anas who spent all his waking hours writing what he saw. After the death of Muhammad, Anas was most popularly called upon to clarify what was meant in a particular document. When questioned, Anas would unroll the scrolls to report, 'These are the sayings of the Prophet that I have noted and also read out to him to correct my mistakes.'

All the writing during Muhammad's lifetime was done either on papyrus, palm fibres, bone tablets, hides, white stones or parchment. Incidents were also narrated aloud from memory. Muhammad commanded that the search for knowledge was a sacred duty imposed upon every Muslim. 'Go in search of knowledge even to China,' is a saying commonly repeated in every enlightened Muslim home. Muhammad also said that God has not created anything more perfect or more beautiful than reason and many Muslim children grow up on the maxim that the most excellent jihad is the conquest of the self.

After his message spread beyond Arabia there was great curiosity about Muhammad. Many myths started to circulate about him, some true and some only a figment of people's fantasies. His learned followers started a branch of studies that was called the science of biography. A special group of scholars sat down to scientifically segregate the great volume of information into two categories: authentic and fabricated. Imam Bukhari, a famous compiler of narrations who died in 870 AD, had in his collection six million documents out of which he accepted only 7275 as authentic and put

The Science of Biography

them together in a book called *Sahih Bukhari*.

Imam Muslim, who died five years later, waded through three million narrations but rejected all except 9200 that are available in a publication called *Sahih Muslim*. The other compilers of authentic narrations are Shamail Trimidhi, Ibn Majah, Abu Daud and An-Nisai.

Trimidhi reports that Muhammad's face was genial, but at times when he was deep in thought there were long periods of silence even as he kept himself busy doing something. He did not speak unnecessarily but what he said was always to the point and without any padding. At times he made his meaning clear by slowly repeating what he had said. He mostly smiled. He kept his feelings under firm control. When annoyed, he would turn aside or keep silent, and when pleased, he would lower his eyes.

The Kaaba

The Kaaba has always been a place of solace for Meccans and Muslims around he world. The temple of Mecca stands in the centre of the city. It is a square building in stone with a door on the east side. In the corner next to this door is the sacred black stone complemented by a white stone on the north side of the Kaaba, said to be the sepulchre of Ismail. Apart from three pillars made from aloes wood between which silver lamps hang, the shrine is quite empty inside. The outside has a covering of a rich, black damask cloth embroidered in gold that is changed each year.

It is believed that the sacred black stone, probably a piece of meteorite, had journeyed down a long time ago from above to tie a divine knot of unity between heaven and earth. The square structure at the centre of the shrine was built by Adam to shelter himself and Eve when they realized that they could not live in Paradise anymore. The Kaaba was later rebuilt by Abraham to house his infant son Ismail.

The Biblical story of Abraham's sacrifice of Isaac from his wife Sarah is different to the one believed by Muslims. In a dream when Abraham is asked by God to sacrifice his beloved son, it is Ismail from his Egyptian wife Hajara who is led to the altar. But as he is about to strike Ismail after having bound his hands and feet and laid him down on the altar, a voice explains to Abraham that it was not the will of God to see Ismail killed. A black and white sheep that had been pasturing for forty years in paradise appeared for the sacrifice instead, and Ismail, on whose life were depended such important events to come, left the place.

Ismail is the ancestor of Arab Muslims and every sheep sacrificed by more than a billion Muslims around the world on Id-ul-Adha is in commemoration of that great sacrifice and for the long life granted to Ismail. The feast of Adha—literally meaning sheep, goats or other cattle reared as a sacrifice to God—is held annually at the end of the Hajj to this day.

It was almost 2793 years before the beginning of the Islamic calendar in 622 AD that Sarah is reported to have become jealous of Hajara and Ismail. She did not want them to live in the same house as her. Abraham left Syria and brought the mother and son to Mecca, described at that time as a barren and empty desert utterly devoid of water and vegetation. Later Ismail helped him to build the Kaaba again under the guidance of angel Gabriel.

In the Koran, it says, 'And remember when Abraham raised the foundation of the House with Ismail, praying, "Our Lord! Accept, this service, from us."

'And remember when we made the House a resort for mankind and a sanctuary saying, "Take ye the station of Abraham a place of prayer for you; and covenated with Abraham and Ismail saying, purify ye two my house for those who make circuit, and for those who prostrate in adoration."'

From this verse Muslims receive the purpose of the Kaaba, and its relevance is revealed to them in another Koranic verse that quotes Abraham as saying, 'O Our Lord! Verily I have housed a part of my offspring in a

The Kaaba

valley uncultivated, nigh unto thy holy house, our Lord! That they may establish prayer; so make thou the hearts of some of the people yearn unto them! And provide them with fruits, that they may be grateful.'

When the custodianship of the Kaaba was entrusted to the Kuraish they guarded the place with their heart and soul and sincerely believed that it was their devotion to the Kaaba that was responsible for their personal prosperity. However, a long time ago the Kaaba was the domain of the tribe of Jurhum and later passed into the hands of the Khuzaa. It was towards the end of the fifth century that Qusayy, the patriarch of the Kuraish tribe, travelled down from somewhere in the northwest lands of Arabia (present day Jordan) to take control over the Kaaba, then home of Hubal, the god of the Khuzaa tribe. It is believed that Qusayy may have also brought with him the cult of two other goddesses and placed the idols beside Hubal at the Kaaba.

Each day was such a struggle for survival for the Arabs that the water and shade of the Kaaba served as a welcome respite from the rat race. In between all the buying and selling, the Arabs were happy to disarm themselves of all vendetta and competition at the Kaaba. The time spent here was used to rest and recreate for a while.

The Five Pillars of Islam

All that Muhammad did in his life was to try and strike a balance between the spiritual, economic and political ambitions of man. He tried to purify the religion of his time that meant not merely rituals but a living, practising way of life to him, and he waged war against corruption and infidelity. He claimed no superhuman powers and said, 'I am only a warner, and a herald of glad tidings to people who believe.'

Muhammad did not claim to be saying anything new but only reminding the Arabs who had forgotten the belief of their forefathers like Abraham in one God.

And to get people to believe in what he was saying he tried to do so by setting an example in all aspects of his own life, from ethical conduct to diet, under the direct guidance of God, that ultimate idea of perfection and goodness. To be a Muslim in short is simply to be good. And the five pillars of Islam are basic religious duties that are meant to help Muslims be good human beings.

Tawhid

The concept of *tawhid*, or the oneness of God, is the soul of Islam, and it is celebrated in just four lines in the Koran where God is extolled as Al-Ahad, the One, as As-Samad, the eternal, as One who does not give birth and One who is born to none. To Muhammad this short verse known as Al-Ikhlas was as good as one-third of the spirit of the entire Koran.

Tawhid is also the religion's first pillar, and *shahada* is the declaration of faith that there is no god but God.

The declaration of the oneness of God and acceptance that Muhammad is the messenger to oneself from the bottom of the heart is the first step to being a Muslim.

Even the ancient Arabs did not have to be coaxed by Muhammad into believing in one God. They already agreed that the supreme deity of the entire family of hundreds of idols was Al-Lah (God). But the Meccans were distracted from the devotion to the supreme God due to their attraction to a host of other idols, making the monotheistic Jews and Christians rebuke and taunt them about their pagan ways. Muhammad's spiritual quest led him back to his Semitic roots or to the straight path. He dwelt upon the unwavering devotion of Abraham to one God and was inspired to do the same.

He never once claimed that he was founding a new religion nor attempted to call it after himself. He insisted that he was only seeking a way to the right path, for those who were lost. Muhammad is described as a serious, introspective young man who was uncomfortable with the act of pagan worship, practised with such aplomb by the Meccan society. He seemed more attracted to the ways of the saintly and very reclusive Hanifs, who believed in the one God of Abraham, although they did not follow Judaism or Christianity, the two monotheistic religions already in practice in the area. The Hanifs pined for an experience of God without the help of middlemen like miracle-makers or idols.

According to historians, many Arabs in the seventh century were turning away from the worship of wealth and polytheism. A further quest had begun for something more wholesome and more meaningful than mere mercantile success. The birth of the founder of Islam most certainly coincided with the spiritual restlessness in the very bosom of the barren lands of the Arabian Peninsula. The abstract ideas of infinity and the endless cycle of birth and death debated by monotheists introduced into the materialistic Meccan mind the exciting new concept of the cycle of life. What fired the imagination of the young and restless at heart were religious ideas pouring in from outside the Hijaz about life beyond the material world. These thoughts made the eternal fate of the individual sound far more precious than it seemed within the tribal society.

Many Arabs were attracted to the monotheism of Christianity, but numerous Christian sects that the Bedouin encountered in different parts of the peninsula in the seventh century confused him. For example, the majestic Christian church at Najran in the south was a source of endless wonder, but in the end the Arab did not quite trust the religious systems and vowed to remain independent of them. His own identity was precious to him and he desperately wanted to preserve and protect it. The Koran is considered very precious as God is at last seen to address the Arab in his own language through the holy text.

In fact to this day all tribal society remains suspicious of large and formal institutions, state structures and centralized governments that comprise people who are not one of their own. Yet it also feels a sense of inferiority, both spiritually and politically, in comparison to more inclusive and cosmopolitan cultures and societies. Just before Muhammad's message stirred the imagination of the Meccans, someone called Maslama had preached in the name of one God he called Rahman or the merciful. Muhammad Ibn Ishaq (who died in 767 AD), one of the Prophet's first biographers, writes that more and more Arabs felt that the religion of their ancestor Abraham was corrupted and that the act of going around the stone at the Kaaba seemed devoid of meaning. 'Find yourselves a religion, for by God, you have none,' one Arab had chided his fellow tribesmen in pre-Islamic times.

Zayd ibn Amr is remembered for refusing to worship the idols of the founders of his tribe and for being openly critical of all pagan rituals. Standing by the Kaaba, Zayd had regretted in a loud voice, 'Oh God, if I knew how you wished to be worshipped I would so worship you; but I do not know.' Zayd had to flee Mecca from all those who were devoted to idol worship, and for many years he wandered far and wide in search of true faith. Then he met a monk in either Syria or Iraq who told him about Muhammad and his message about one God. But before Zayd could return home to meet Muhammad and celebrate the discovery of the kind of spirituality he was looking for, he was killed. Later Syed, his son, grew up to become one of Muhammad's most trusted companions.

The question that ate away at the soul of the new age thinkers, especially those who had traded the pastoral nomadic life for a sedentary one in the city, was how to find a way to put into practice the attractive, new concept of individualism or the holistic being without undermining the communal ethos. After all, both the tribal system and the old paganism had served the Bedouin well for centuries, but now life was tossing and turning in anticipation of tumultuous changes that would eventually wake up not just the Arabs but also societies asleep around the world. Muhammad's message of one God integrated the Arabs without challenging their independence and identity.

Namaz

The daily prayer, performed five times during the day, is the second pillar of Islam. The ritual prostration and other gestures during prayer are as important as the mental activity. The Muslims are called upon to: 'Give glory to God when you reach eventide and when you rise in the morning, to Him be praise in the heavens and on earth and in the late afternoon and when the day begins to decline.'

Muslims always face the Kaaba while offering the prayer in whichever part of the world they might be. This was not always so. Before his discourses with friendly Arab Jews in Medina, the favourite prophet of Muhammad was Moses and all worship was performed in the qibla or direction of Jerusalem. After he left Mecca, Muhammad replaced the importance of Moses in the lives of Muslims with Abraham, the father of Ismail, making Islam independent of the older faith of Judaism. Some eighteen months after his arrival in Medina, while he led the prayers in the mosque, he made the entire congregation turn away from Jerusalem and pray towards the Kaaba.

The prayer can be offered without any supervision from a priest for the only witness that a Muslim requires is one's own conscience and the only obligation is to remain pure at heart and intention. That is the only way to get close to God and the daily prayer is a symbolic communion similar to Muhammad's meeting with God during the Miraj or Ascension, the mystical journey he made beyond the seven heavens. The ritual performed five times each day is a divine gift that Muhammad brought back from this journey that occurred at a time when Muhammad struggled to come to terms with perhaps the saddest period in his life. He was on the run from the Meccan warlords who threatened to kill him. Also, he was very lonely as Abu Talib and Khadija were both dead.

Under these circumstances the journey to heaven seemed like a favour granted by God to light up Muhammad's life. He had a vision that he travelled from Mecca to Jerusalem, and led by Gabriel he ascended one by one each of the seven heavens. At every station he met the earlier prophets—Moses, Jesus, Abraham and Adam—and beyond the seventh heaven he passed through multiple veils that concealed what is hidden. Once he reached the veil of unity he was rewarded with a vision of what the eye is unable to see and the mind cannot imagine. In the Koran a verse describes God as light, 'God is the Light of the heavens and the earth; the likeness of His Light is as a niche wherein is a lamp, the lamp in a glass that is like a glittering star, kindled from a Blessed Tree, an olive that is neither of the East nor of the West, whose oil well nigh would shine, even if no fire touched it; Light upon Light' (Koran 24:35).

In a place where water was scarce, Muhammad made it mandatory for Muslims to clean themselves, even if it was just with a bowlful of water, before reaching out to think of God. He owned very few clothes but he was very particular about cleanliness. He liked others to be simply dressed in clean clothes. Muhammad would say, 'Cleanliness is piety,' and when he came across someone with dirty clothes he would ask, 'Why can't this man wash them?'

Zakat

This is the compulsory act of alms-giving or charity, and if practised liberally, is the answer to end that yawning gap of economic disparity between people. Muhammad always shared whatever he had with those who had even less. Even before he declared Islam as a formal religion he was an enthusiastic member of an order of chivalry founded by his elders to address grievances of the oppressed, whether they were residents of Mecca or visitors. He kept his pledge never to give up his involvement with this order even if a herd of camels were offered to him. Throughout his life he maintained that if somebody appealed to him any time, by the virtue of that pledge he would hurry to help.

Once he began to preach publicly, Muhammad stressed the obligation of the rich to the poor and made it a duty for Muslims to give on a regular basis without motive, for God says, 'Do not nullify your charity by reminders of your generosity, or by holding it against those you give it to, like those who give their wealth only to be seen by others . . . They are like hard, barren rock on which is little soil. Heavy rain falls on it and leaves it just a bare stone.' Any charitable work done with the intention to show off one's generosity has no relevance.

Just like there is no priest watching over a Muslim perform worship, so also there is no authority that can force a Muslim to perform charity. Muhammad's prophecy remains a combination of genuine respect for individualism and regard for the welfare of the community as a whole. He always identified with those who did not have much and prayed that he would remain poor in life. After death he asked God to raise him at resurrection among the poor.

He believed that nothing is ever held against the weak and the sick or against those that find nothing to spend, provided that they are true to God. His wife Aisha said that there was no type of work that was too lowly for Muhammad. He always helped her in the house, mending his own clothes, repairing shoes and sweeping the floor. He would milk, tether and feed the animals, and do the shopping. Muhammad defined charity as any act that brings about a just reconciliation between two contestants—helping a person mount his animal or to load his baggage onto it is charity, a good word is charity, to remove obstacles in the street is charity, smiling upon the face of your brother is charity, sexual relations with your spouse is charity, and so on.

From a hut he built of unbaked clay with his own hands and thatched with palm leaves and camel skin, Muhammad would say that it is difficult for a man laden with riches to climb the steep path that leads to bliss.

He was once offered a softer bed instead of the rope cot that he slept on, and he declined, saying, 'What have I to do with worldly things. My connection with the world is like that of a traveller resting for a while underneath the shade of a tree and then moving on.'

Roza

The fourth pillar of Islam is the obligatory fasting from sunrise to sunset during Ramadan, the ninth month of the Islamic calendar, mainly to practice self-restraint. Muhammad wanted to share with everyone the precious experience of being cleansed spiritually when he meditated in the mountains. Ever since he was a child, Muhammad was in the habit of retiring for the entire month of Ramadan to caves in the mountains just like his grandfather Abdul Muttalib. After he declared Islam a formal way of life, he hoped that others would also experience the nearness he felt to God each time he was able to concentrate only on the Creator, leaving all thoughts of worldly excitement behind him.

However if negative thoughts and feelings like hate, anger and greed remain in the heart then the ritual at Ramadan becomes meaningless. It is said in the Koran, 'There are many who fast all day and pray all night, but they gain nothing but hunger and sleeplessness.'

Hajj

Hajj is the pilgrimage to the Kaaba. Dr Ali Shariati, the Iranian philosopher, explains the Hajj to the Kaaba as the non-station of devotees. The Hajj to the holy shrine is not the final destination but a sign showing that the way is not lost, that the believer is on the right path. Kept in the niche of the eastern wall of the Kaaba is the black stone which had fallen from heaven in the primeval days of Adam. The void is the negation of all human attempts to define the divine and black indicates the blinding glory of God wrapped in its own concentrated radiance. The space within the cube which is devoid of any ornamentation is symbolic of the secret of God in the universe, for God remains shapeless, colourless and without any form or condition selected up to this day by mankind. Whatever is imagined so far as God, is not God.

The Kaaba, as the earthly home of God, is a replica of the world itself, each corner of the cube arising from one central point of gravity. Starting from the eastern corner of the cube beside the sacred black stone, Muslims circle the Kaaba seven times in the same way that the earth goes around the sun. This is a ritual that is common to nearly all cultures and is symbolic of the infinite aspect of both, the nature of the world and the depths of the human psyche. The circumambulations perfect the square within a circle pattern. With its four axes, the square is an expression of the solidity of the earth confined within the spatiality of the heavenly sphere represented by the circle. With each return to the start while circling around the Kaaba, the pilgrim is expected to live the truth that in every repeated return to the start is also a new beginning.

To perform the Hajj is to remember God's forgiveness of Adam and Eve, to be grateful for the long life of Ismail and to celebrate the presence of Muhammad in our midst. Above all, the pilgrimage is performed in the hope of instilling in the self a sense of everlasting modesty and humility as the ego is seen to surrender itself into nothing at the altar of God, the only truth and ultimate reality.

The Message of the Koran

In its own words, 'The Koran is God's speech and therefore sacred and the truth. The Koran is sent down to make everything clear (Koran 16:89).'

The message of the Koran is that God exists. The God who exists is great because he is the master of the universe. God is also merciful and compassionate and will help all those who believe, trust and surrender themselves to God to keep on the straight path. Those who keep to the straight path are blessed by God, but anger is directed against those who have gone astray and wander in the wilderness. On the day of judgement, God will condemn all those that have strayed to a terrible fate, and the faithful, the believers and the friends of God will be vindicated.

Although believers are told to prepare for the day of judgement, it is also stressed that, 'There is nothing but our present life, we die and we live and nothing but time destroys us' (Koran 45:24).

Between the positive of those who believe and the negative of those who do not is the endless possibility for the two extremes to meet and for all those who are lost to return to the straight path under the guidance of prophets like Muhammad. The merciful God does provide divine guidance but in the end it is left to the individual to decide which path to tread. Muhammad is told by God to tell human beings, 'Say, the truth is from your Lord so let whosoever will believe and let whosoever will disbelieve.'

The majority of Bedouins communicated with each other orally. It is not surprising that when God chose to speak to the Arabs through Muhammad it was done through a series of recitations in the Arabic language that came to the Messenger of God verse by verse over a period of two decades and especially in moments when Muhammad looked for divine guidance for problems he faced in society. The Arabs were in the habit of memorizing everything by heart. The entire Koranic text of 77,000 words, 114 chapters and 6236 verses interlock into each other in a rhythmic structure and is memorized and recited by people to this day. In earlier times, only a *hafiz* or an expert memorized the Koran, and when he died in war it was feared that the recitations might be lost. That is when a single unified text was compiled, perhaps the first written text in the Arabic language.

The fact that Muhammad did not read or write is emphasized by Muslims today also as a symbol of the purity of his heart and soul. Islamic sources describe a process of revelations that were oral and piecemeal, and brought to Muhammad from God by the angel Gabriel. It is reported that Muhammad sometimes saw the angel in the form of a human being and sometimes only sensed the presence of the heavenly body. Sometimes the recitations were lucid and clear and at other times Muhammad had to decipher sounds and visions and recite the revelations to his companions who wrote them down.

The verses revealed to Muhammad in Mecca are more abstract and establish his credentials as the Prophet. And all the verses that tell of the duties and norms of behaviour in daily life came to Muhammad in

Medina as he built the foundations of the ideal Muslim society. While the Meccan verses are considered to be the more poetic ones, those revealed in Medina are largely prosaic in comparison.

Muslims take guidance from the Koran, the source of which is God. The example set by Muhammad is known as the Sunnah of the Prophet. Often his companions would ask him to clarify if at a particular time he was conveying the will of God or his personal view. When it was his own view, he allowed it to be debated and often suggestions of his companions were allowed to supersede his own opinion.

Once a man slapped his wife and she came to complain to Muhammad. He was about to have the husband slapped in retribution when God intervened and sent the controversial verse, 'Men are the managers of the affairs of women for that God has preferred one of them over another, and for that they have expended of their property. Righteous women are therefore obedient, guarding the secret for God's guarding. And those you fear may be rebellious admonish; banish them to their couches and beat them. If they then obey you, look not for any way against them; God is All-high, All-great' (Koran 4:34). Muhammad replied that he had wanted one thing but God willed another.

The Last Sermon

The Last Sermon

In 631 AD after performing Hajj for the last time, Muhammad spoke to 124,000 Muslims from Mount Arafat.

He said, 'Oh people, lend me an attentive ear. I know not whether after this year I shall ever be amongst you again.

'Oh people, just as you regard this month, this day, this city as sacred, so regard the life and property of every Muslim as a sacred trust. Return the goods entrusted to you to their rightful owners.

'Hurt no one so that no one may hurt you.

'Do not take usury, this is forbidden to you.

'Aid the poor and clothe them as you would clothe yourselves.

'Remember! One day you will appear before Allah and answer for your deeds. So, beware! Do not stray from the path of righteousness after I am gone.

'Oh people! No prophet or apostle will come after me and no new faith will be born . . . It is true that you have certain rights with regard to your own women, but they also have rights over you. Treat them well for they are your support.

'Reflect on my words. I leave behind two things, the Koran and my example, and if you follow these guides you will not fail.

'Listen to me in earnest. Worship God, say your prayers, fast during the months of Ramadan, and give your wealth in charity.

'All the believers are brothers. All have the same rights and same responsibilities.

'No one is allowed to take from another what he does not allow him of his own free will. None is higher than the other unless he is higher in virtue.

'All those who listen to me shall pass on my words to others, and those to others again, and may the last ones understand my words better than those who listen to me directly.'

Muhammad then turned his face towards the heavens and said, 'Be my witness, Oh Allah, that I have conveyed your message to your people.'

And from the foothills of Arafat the united voice of thousands of Muslims echoed, 'My Lord, surely you have.'

After Muhammad

The root of Muhammad's revolution lay in very conventional morality and he made moral discovery the main quest of his life. Muhammad forever inspired all those around him by pointing out that if he was able to realize the goodness within himself it was also easy for everyone else to do the same.

While Muhammad perfected the art of being good, most of his followers continue to struggle with evil. Unable to fathom the veracity of the truth Muhammad talked about, his followers fight each other trying to imitate him in attire and physical appearance alone. Muhammad surrendered to none other than God but over the millennia Muslims have learnt to pay homage to monarchs and allowed themselves to be ruled often by the most miserable of men.

> Look, your homeland is the land of Islam, and what do you find there? A tyrannical ruler who rules to please himself, so where is the moral basis? Men of religion who bring religion into subjection to serve the ruler, so where is the moral basis? And a people who think only of the morsel which will fill their stomachs, so where is the moral basis?
>
> —In *The Journey of Ibn Fattouma*, a novel by Naquib Mahfouz

There seems little moral basis in any land of Islam today as more Muslims perhaps want to moralize and not enough of them are moral. Muslims look upon Muhammad for inspiration but his way of life was so simple that they find it the most difficult example to follow.

During his last days Muhammad left the decision of leadership to his followers. After his death, a constitutional assembly unanimously elected Abu Bakr, one of his closest companions and father-in-law, as head of Medina's Muslim community. During the two years that he was at the helm of affairs, Abu Bakr won over some of the most rebellious tribes and quelled revolts with great wisdom to keep all of Arabia united.

Consultations were held after the death of the able and elderly Abu Bakr with other companions of Muhammad and Omar was chosen as successor. Omar, a distant relative and once bitterly opposed to Muhammad, converted to Islam after he heard Muhammad reciting from the Koran. The sheer sound of the words so melted his heart that he surrendered immediately. Omar said that Muhammad had used the Arabic language in such a poetic way that it pierced through all his prejudices and stirred his soul. 'When I heard the Koran my heart was softened and I wept, and Islam entered into me,' Omar confessed about his conversion.

Omar governed for ten years and under his leadership Muslim armies marched into Iraq, Syria and Egypt. Jerusalem was conquered and became the third holy city in the Islamic world after Mecca and Medina. Omar is responsible for bringing the Persian Empire to its knees but he was later killed by a Persian prisoner of war. In his lifetime, he had established an electoral council of seven elders to decide a successor.

According to Karen Armstrong there was nothing religious about the Muslim wars of expansion. 'Omar did not believe that he had a divine mandate to conquer the world. The objective of Omar and his warriors was entirely pragmatic: they wanted plunder and a common activity that would preserve the unity of the community. For centuries the Arabs had tried to raid the richer settled lands beyond the peninsula; the difference was that this time they had encountered a power vacuum,' explains Armstrong in *A Short History of Islam*.

In *Muhammad for Beginners*, authors Ziauddin Sardar and Zafar Abbas Malik point out that Abu Bakr realized that the young Muslim state was eyed as a juicy morsel by Rome and Iran. He sent an ambassador to Constantinople to seek a peaceful solution but Byzantium's emperor Heraclius did not respond in kind forcing Muslims to capture one city after another in both Syria and Iraq.

Syed Amir Ali in *The Spirit of Islam* writes that in turning their arms against Persia the Muslims were led by circumstances. It was the semi Arab kings, ruling under the shadow of Persian monarchs, that got involved in hostilities with Muslims who in their new found strength under a single ruler for the first time in Arab history fought back with ferocity and easily won over powers exhausted from centuries of fighting with each other. The Muslim armies won the hearts of the people as they were treated with respect and kindness. Omar made sure that the conquered lands were not divided among the soldiers but remained with the peasants who paid taxes to the Muslim state. The soldiers lived without pomp, upholding family values, and drunkenness was not tolerated. Omar was a great promoter of the simple virtues of Muhammad and himself lived a frugal life. He was a leader whose greatest concern remained the ethical progress of his followers who were impressed by the personal example set by Omar more than his word. At this time Islam was seen purely as an Arab religion and non-Arabs were not expected to become Muslims.

After the assassination of Omar, Osman ruled and remains the most controversial leader of the community. He belonged to the affluent merchant family of Omayya that was in opposition to the Hashim family of Muhammad, two clans, both offshoots from the common tribe of Kuraish. Osman was also a son-in-law of Muhammad. He ruled for twelve years when Cyprus and Tripoli surrendered and the Muslims ruled Iran, Afghanistan and Sind in the Indian subcontinent.

But piety seemed to find it difficult to keep pace with the rapid expansion of territory and Osman was accused of nepotism. The Muslims of Medina complained that Osman favoured people from his own family for the most plum posts that were created everyday as Islam spread far and wide. Eventually Osman was murdered in 656 AD and Ali was the fourth in line, and last of the leadership considered devout, after Muhammad. In less than five years Ali was also murdered, after having fought and won the famous Battle of the Camel against none other than Aisha, Muhammad's youngest wife.

Abu Dhar Ghafari is the first critic of the community of Muslims. One of Muhammad's closest companions, Abu Dhar stayed out of all the contests for power and was distressed to watch believers slip into deep decadence so soon after the death of Muhammad. Before he came to live with Muhammad, Abu Dhar was a half savage and a notorious warrior from the dreaded Ghafar tribe that roamed the lands of the Waddan Valley between Mecca and Medina. His only job was to loot caravans for a living. It was his habit to force ransom from caravans and used the worst kind of force against those who refused to pay. One day Abu Dhar received news of the gentle ways of Muhammad brought to him on the shoulders of a sandstorm. His conscience corroded and an inner voice forbid Abu Dhar from bullying and terrorizing people weaker than himself.

He laid down his sword and wandered in search of Muhammad. On meeting him Abu Dhar spontaneously said, *as salaam alaikum* oh Muhammad, or peace be upon you, and Muhammad replied *walaikum as salaam*, or peace upon you too. That day Abu Dhar renounced all violence and at the peak of his strength became one of Muhammad's most sedate companions.

Now he cried out from his mud dwelling to Muhammad's successors not to hoard gold and silver but to equally divide it amongst all Muslims. Abu Dhar believed passionately that Islam was the refuge of the helpless and the oppressed. He was critical of wealth spent on building palaces while people had little to eat. He continued to gather the humiliated and the needy around him, rallying them against usury, money-worshippers, gold gatherers and aristocrats. He reminded them of Abu Bakr who had earned his living in Medina by milking goats for a Jewish family and chided Osman with, 'Oh Osman, you have made the poor, poor and the wealthy, wealthy.

'If you are building this palace with your own money, it is extravagance, and if with the money of the people, it is treason,' he warned. And complaining that he could no longer live beside those who loved gold and silver more than human beings, Abu Dhar left both Medina and Damascus one day to live out the rest of his life far away from opulence in a corner of the desert.

The incident of Karbala (Southern Iraq) involving Husain, a grandson of Muhammad and the son of Ali and Fatima, is the earliest and most poignant of protests against the wayward ways of Muslim rulers of that time. Just half a century after Muhammad's death, Husain led a caravan of family and friends towards the garrison town of Kufa to join a people's uprising against the unjust ways of the authorities. Husain was armed with little else except his grandfather's teachings and was stopped at Karbala where water was denied to him and to his companions. Husain was the last one killed with his infant son in his arms.

Over time the tragedy at Karbala has grown into a cult and has made a powerful niche in the psyche and personal life of those Muslims opposed to tyranny and injustice. Muslims around the world even to this day mourn the martyrdom of Husain every Ashura, the tenth day of Muharram, the first month of the Islamic calendar. However, the fact that many Muslims who weep, beat their bodies and continue to flagellate themselves in frustration have forgotten why they repeat the ritual annually is another story.

Dynastic rule was declared in Damascus as early as 661 AD, ending the originally democratic and accountable spirit of Islam. But a golden era dawned between 750 AD and 1258 AD with the rise of the Abbasid rulers from the family of Muhammad's uncle, Abbas. The capital was moved from Damascus to Kufa in Iraq. The city of Baghdad was founded in 765 AD as the seat of Darul as-salam or the abode of peace and remained an undisputed spiritual and temporal authority for five centuries during which time the local population was involved in translating into Arabic the classical Greek texts on philosophy and medical science. It was a period of peace and great cultural renaissance. Although autocratic, the Abbasids attained a zenith of prosperity that was unrivalled.

The spread of Islam was so wide that by the tenth century no single city could claim to be its capital. Cordova was a thriving capital and a member of the house of Ali, and Fatima took Egypt and Syria from the Abbasids to create the Fatimid dynasty and also founded Cairo's al-Azhar University in 970 AD.

A line of unelected monarchs continued to establish dynasties from Armenia to Andalusia, bringing half the then known world under Muslim rule. From its desert origins Islam became a world civilization. Its success lay in allowing the people it conquered to live in peace and to practice their own religion after they were liberated from the distant and often cruel domination of several previous kings. Islamic rulers shared learning with their subjects and borrowed hungrily from other civilizations, including Babylonian, Chinese, Egyptian, Greek, Indian and Persian.

Between 750 AD and 1492 AD Muslim Spain became history's first multi-religious and multicultural society and all arguments and debates within societies everywhere flooded out of the mosque on to crossroads and into institutions. Along with the study of sciences and the arts, scholars like Ibn Sulaiman also gave tips on *How An Old Man Can Become Young Again*, published in the fifteenth century.

Islam's lamp of learning glowed so bright from the seventh century that it lighted up other continents as well, including Europe that was cloaked then in a coarse thicket spun around it by the Dark Ages. However, even as Europe basked in a new Renaissance, the Muslims gradually seemed to forget what they had taught other people. As the morality of monarchs meandered, religious leaders jumped in to rescue the community in the seventeenth century. They resolved the crisis by banning all learning and confining the community only to religious knowledge. The famed practice of consensus by the community was reduced to a council only of religious leaders. And silence was imposed upon all independent understanding and reasoning enjoyed by Muslims for nearly a thousand years.

The first set back to Islam came in 1258 when the Mongols attacked Baghdad and thirty-six public libraries were sacked and set on fire. Dressed in the black mantle of the Abbasids, the rulers were forced to flee to Cairo in 1261 and lived there as religious heads. At the beginning of the sixteenth century the decadent rulers of Cairo were overthrown by Selim from the clan of Osman to found the Ottoman dynasty, making Constantinople the capital, and renaming it Islambol or the city of Islam.

Fascinated by the spectacular spread of Islam and then its decline, Ibn Khaldun, the fourteenth century Muslim philosopher and statesman, tried to explain how a luxurious life is able to blind the senses and stagnate growth. His book *Al Muqaddimah*, 'The Introduction to History', makes Khaldun the world's first social scientist and his theory is still considered a most helpful way of understanding societies. Khaldun says that states rise and fall due to the constant replacement of the ruling class by conquering nomads from the periphery of the presidential palace. Once the invaders settle down and have lost the skills of life picked up in the wilderness they themselves become slack, confined as they are in the centre of the city. That is the time for the next round of raw energy to replace the overripe and rotting elite.

According to Khaldun's theory the Roman Empire had stood helpless against the more vigorous assault of Germanic tribes that took over the indulgent and comfortable life of men in imperial cities. The Arabs too found it easy to overrun the decadent empires of Byzantium and Persia. And later the Mongols under the leadership of Genghis Khan thundered into the world of Islam made effeminate after years of living a sedentary life of abundance, to create a brand new lineage of nobility. Ibn Khaldun also noted that the larger a dynasty the longer it took to collapse. He writes that the real reason why large dynasties last longer is because collapse begins in far away regions and each defection takes time to travel to the centre.

Once in Europe, Islam made both friend and foe. While Islam was embraced by some, other Europeans first denounced it as far back as in the ninth century. During the bloody Crusades or the 100-year war between Islam and Christianity, Muhammad was portrayed as anti-Christ and a defamatory character of Muhammad became part of a cycle of popular performances based on Chanson literature. But apart from intense propaganda by others, a love of luxuries, intrigues, numerous internal feuds and the break up of the community into various sects is also something that does not do Islam proud today.

It is the fall of Granada in 1492 that is really marked by historians as the beginning of the end of the glorious period of Islamic rule in Spain, also considered to be the most enlightened. As Boadbil's mother had watched the

Moorish Prince of Granada kneel before King Ferdinand and surrender the key to the city, she had cried out, 'You weep like a woman for what you could not hold as a man.'

The scene was repeated four centuries later as Wajid Ali Shah, the last ruler of the United Provinces of central India, put his hands to the crown, glittering with the rarest of rare jewels, to lift it off his head and gift it in 1856 to Sir James Outram, a British general.

It may not be that impossible after all to regain at least some of the dignity lost over time but only if every Muslim first makes moral values the most meaningful aspect of his life. Just like Muhammad.